Ninja Foodi Digital Air Fryer Oven Cookbook 2024

Easy & Delicious Recipes - All Functions Including Air Crisp, Broil, Toast, Dehydrate to Bake and Roast! Suitable for Beginners and Advanced Chefs

Jared Rodgers

CONTENTS

INTRODUCTION

Welcome to the exciting world of the Ninja Foodi Digital Air Fryer Oven, where cooking becomes an enjoyable experience! This versatile appliance is perfect for both experienced chefs and beginners, making your experience easier and sparking creativity in every dish.

The Ninja Foodi is a versatile cooking companion that allows you to bake, roast, air fry, dehydrate, and more. Its versatile features allow you to experiment with different cooking techniques and create a wide range of delicious dishes using just one appliance. The Foodi effortlessly handles a wide range of dishes, from crispy breakfasts to succulent main courses and decadent desserts.

I initially had doubts when I brought the Ninja Foodi Digital Air Fryer Oven into my kitchen. Can this modern appliance truly replace multiple kitchen tools that I hold dear? The Foodi quickly became the focal point of my culinary adventures.

I decided to test the Foodi by making a delicious one-pot chicken casserole recipe. I was pleasantly relieved by how little time it took to prepare, and how little effort was required during the cooking process. What is the outcome? A delicious meal that received high praise from even the most critical judges—my children.

As you explore and try new things, you'll be amazed by the endless possibilities of the Ninja Foodi. You're enjoying making homemade pizzas, baking tasty treats, and even dehydrating nutritious snacks for the kids. With this appliance, you can replace multiple gadgets and enjoy the freedom to explore your culinary skills without the inconvenience of using and cleaning numerous tools.

Discover the wonders of the Ninja Foodi with this comprehensive cookbook, designed to help you navigate your own culinary adventure. It's packed with recipes, ranging from simple and convenient meals to impressive dishes that you'll be delighted to showcase. Discover the joy and satisfaction of cooking with this incredible appliance through helpful tips, tricks, and easy-to-follow step-by-step instructions. Prepare yourself for a journey into the world of tantalizing flavors as you begin this culinary adventure with your trusty Ninja Foodi. Discover new taste combinations, try innovative cooking techniques, and above all, savor the joy of crafting mouthwatering dishes. It's a world where cooking is enjoyable, simple, and incredibly satisfying.

Benefits of Using a Digital Air Fryer Oven

The Ninja Foodi Digital Air Fryer Oven is a revolutionary addition to any kitchen. This compact device combines multiple cooking functions, offering numerous benefits that make cooking a breeze, promote better health, and enhance the overall cooking experience. Discover the numerous advantages of incorporating a digital air fryer oven into your kitchen:

- **Healthier Cooking**
  One significant advantage of using a digital air fryer oven is the ability to make healthier meals easily. Conventional frying methods often involve using substantial quantities of oil, adding excessive fat and calories to your food. Using the air fryer function, you can easily achieve a crispy texture and mouthwatering taste with minimal or no oil required. You can savor all your beloved fried dishes, like fries, chicken wings, and onion rings, without feeling guilty.
- **Versatility**
  The Ninja Foodi Digital Air Fryer Oven is a multifunctional powerhouse. It can air fry, bake, roast, broil, dehydrate, and even toast, all in one appliance. This versatility allows you to experiment with various cooking methods and recipes, from crispy snacks to tender roasts and delectable baked goods. Whether you're making breakfast, lunch, dinner, or dessert, this appliance has you covered.
- **Time Efficiency**
  The digital air fryer oven cooks food faster than traditional ovens and stovetops thanks to its rapid air circulation technology and high heat. This means you can get dinner on the table quicker, which is especially beneficial on busy weeknights. Additionally, the preheating time is much shorter, saving you even more time in the kitchen.
- **Energy Efficiency**
  Using a digital air fryer oven can be more energy-efficient than using a conventional oven. Since it heats up quickly and cooks food faster, it uses less energy overall. This not only helps reduce your energy bills but also makes it an environmentally friendly choice.
- **Ease of Use**
  With intuitive digital controls, preset cooking functions, and easy-to-read displays, the Ninja Foodi Digital Air Fryer Oven is user-friendly, even for those who aren't confident in the kitchen. The preset takes the guesswork out of cooking, allowing you to achieve perfect results with the push of a button. Additionally, many models come with helpful accessories, such as racks, trays, and baskets, to enhance your cooking experience.
- **Even Cooking**
  The air fryer oven uses powerful convection fans to circulate hot air around the food, ensuring even cooking and consistent results. This means no more worrying about hotspots or unevenly cooked meals. Whether roasting vegetables or baking cookies, every bite is cooked to perfection.
- **Compact Design**
  Despite its multifunctionality, the digital air fryer oven is compact and takes up less counter space than multiple separate appliances. Its sleek design fits well in any kitchen, and its versatility reduces the need for additional gadgets, decluttering your workspace.
- **Easy Cleanup**
  Cleaning up after cooking can be a chore, but the Ninja Foodi Digital Air Fryer Oven makes it easy. Many parts are dishwasher safe, and the non-stick surfaces prevent food from sticking, making hand washing a breeze. Less oil is used in cooking, so there's also less greasy residue.
- **Consistent Results**
  The air fryer oven guarantees consistent cooking results with its digital precision and reliable performance. Whether you're experimenting with a new recipe or preparing a beloved family dish, rest assured that the Ninja Foodi will consistently produce mouthwatering, flawlessly cooked meals.
- **Cost-Effective**

Choosing a digital air fryer oven can be an intelligent financial choice in the long run. Consolidating multiple functions into one device can result in substantial cost savings on purchasing and maintaining individual appliances. Furthermore, preparing healthy meals at home can save you money by reducing expenses on expensive takeout and dining out.

In general, the Ninja Foodi Digital Air Fryer Oven is a versatile, efficient, and user-friendly appliance that can significantly improve your cooking experience. This product is a valuable asset in any kitchen, making preparing tasty and nutritious meals effortless. Its many advantages make it a great addition to your cooking routine.

Essential Tools and Equipment

To truly master your Ninja Foodi Digital Air Fryer Oven and elevate your cooking experience, it's crucial to equip yourself with the right tools and equipment. This comprehensive list of essentials is designed to enhance your experience with this versatile appliance, making your cooking journey more convenient and enjoyable.

- **Air Fryer Basket**
  The air fryer basket is essential for achieving perfectly crispy and evenly cooked foods such as fries, chicken wings, and vegetables. Its perforated design promotes even air circulation, resulting in a delicious golden-brown finish on your food. Plus, you won't have to use excessive amounts of oil!
  Crisper Plate
- The crisper plate is a game-changer for achieving a delightful crisp on both sides of your food, perfect for air frying. This is particularly handy for smaller items such as tater tots, nuggets, and roasted chickpeas. Its elevated design aids in draining excess oil, ensuring you can enjoy healthier meals without compromising on taste.

Baking Tray

- A baking tray is necessary for creating delicious cookies, sheet cakes, and other baked treats. It ensures that your dough or batter cooks evenly by providing a flat and even surface. Find a non-stick tray to simplify the cleanup process.

Multi-Purpose Rack

- The multi-purpose rack is a testament to the versatility of your Ninja Foodi Digital Air Fryer Oven. It allows you to conveniently cook multiple items simultaneously, making the most of the vertical space in your air fryer oven. This is especially helpful for drying fruits and vegetables, grilling, or cooking multiple pieces of meat at the same time, expanding your cooking horizons and possibilities.

Roasting Pan

- A roasting pan is necessary for preparing larger meals like whole chicken, roasts, and casseroles. The deep sides of this product are designed to contain juices and prevent spills, while also providing enough space for even cooking.

Silicone Baking Mats

- Silicone baking mats are reusable and eco-friendly alternatives to parchment paper. They provide a non-stick surface for baking and roasting, making them ideal for cookies, pastries, and roasted vegetables.

Meat Thermometer

- A meat thermometer is crucial for ensuring your meats are cooked to the proper internal temperature, which is essential for both safety and achieving the perfect level of doneness. With an instant-read digital thermometer, you can get fast and precise readings.

Tongs and Spatulas

- It is crucial to have top-notch tongs and spatulas to ensure the safe flipping and handling of hot food. Tools with silicone tips or made of stainless steel are long-lasting and can withstand high temperatures, which makes them perfect for use with your air fryer oven.

Basting Brushes

- Basting brushes are a convenient way to apply marinades, sauces, and glazes to your food. These silicone brushes are heat-resistant and easily cleaned, making them a practical option for air frying and baking.

Parchment Paper Liners

- Pre-cut parchment paper liners are specially made for air fryer baskets and trays. They make it a breeze to prevent sticking and clean up afterwards. They are particularly useful for baking and cooking sticky or delicate foods.

Oven Mitts and Heat-Resistant Gloves

- It is important to ensure that your hands are well-protected from high temperatures. Consider purchasing a high-quality set of oven mitts or heat-resistant gloves to ensure your safety when handling hot trays, racks, and pans.

Oil Sprayer

- Using an oil sprayer, you can effortlessly coat your food with a delicate oil mist, resulting in a delectably crispy texture while keeping the oil usage in check. For optimal outcomes, seek out a high-quality and refillable sprayer.

Mixing Bowls and Prep Tools

- A collection of mixing bowls and essential prep tools, such as measuring cups, spoons, and a whisk, can significantly simplify your cooking routine. These tools are crucial for preparing ingredients and combining batters or doughs.

Food Storage Containers

- Using airtight food storage containers ensures your leftovers stay fresh. These containers are perfect for meal prepping and ensuring your homemade meals remain tasty and safe to eat for multiple days.

  Cleaning Brushes
- Keeping your air fryer oven and its accessories clean is a breeze with a set of cleaning brushes. This set includes a bottle brush and a detail brush, making it easy to keep everything spotless. Remember, regular cleaning is key to keeping your appliance performing well and lasting a long time, so make it a part of your cooking routine.

Conclusion
Equipping your kitchen with these essential tools and accessories will enhance your Ninja Foodi Digital Air Fryer Oven cooking experience, making it easier, more efficient, and more enjoyable. With the right equipment, you'll be ready to tackle any recipe and make the most of your versatile appliance.

Understanding the Ninja Foodi Functions

The Ninja Foodi Digital Air Fryer Oven is not just an ordinary appliance; it's a versatile culinary tool designed with your ease of use in mind. Despite its many features, navigating the various modes is a breeze. No need to worry, my fellow food enthusiast! This guide will reveal the secrets of each mode, helping you go from a novice to an expert chef with confidence.

Air Frying 101: This takes center stage. Air frying utilizes rapidly circulating hot air to achieve crispy perfection with minimal oil. Imagine French fries that are on par with those made in a deep fryer, succulent chicken wings with crispy skin, and fried vegetables that are both delicious and healthy. Getting the hang of this mode requires grasping the concept of preheating, ensuring even browning by shaking or flipping, and adapting cook times for various ingredients.

Air Roasting: Elevate your roasting skills with air roasting techniques. Like a conventional oven, it utilizes hot air to cook food, but with a quicker and more uniform circulation. This results in beautifully browned meats, perfectly roasted vegetables, and tender, flavorful whole chickens. Try out different temperatures and rack positions to get the results you want.

Air Broiling: Looking to achieve a fast sear or a beautifully caramelized top on your food? Air broiling is the perfect solution. This mode uses a heating element positioned at the top of the oven cavity to provide powerful direct heat. Imagine the delightful sight of perfectly golden brown cheese on casseroles, the irresistible crunch of bacon for breakfast sandwiches, and the mouthwatering appearance of beautifully seared steaks. When air broiling, it's important to keep a close eye on your food to prevent burning.

Baking Like a Boss: The Ninja Foodi is not only great for air frying, but it also excels at baking! The Bake mode utilizes traditional radiant heat to create a consistent cooking environment, ideal for making cakes, cookies, breads, and pastries. Get to know the preheating times and baking temperatures for different recipes to achieve the golden brown results you desire.

Toasting Perfection: With the Toast mode, your breakfast routine becomes a breeze, ensuring perfectly crisp bagels and golden brown toast every time. Customize the level of toasting to suit everyone's preference with adjustable settings. Discover how to easily toast frozen waffles, croutons, and nuts for a fast and nutritious snack.

Dehydrating Delights: Discover the Dehydrate mode to effortlessly preserve the abundance of your garden or whip up nutritious snacks. This mode is perfect for removing moisture from food at a low temperature. You can easily create homemade fruit leathers, jerky, and dried herbs with it. Try out different drying times and temperatures for different ingredients to see what works best.

This is just a glimpse into the many possibilities your Ninja Foodi has to offer. By becoming proficient in these modes and delving into their intricacies, you'll open up a realm of culinary ingenuity and exciting opportunities for experimentation. Alright, gather up your preferred ingredients, select your mode, and prepare to cook with inspiration and excitement!

Maintenance and Cleaning Guide

Proper maintenance and regular cleaning of your Ninja Foodi Digital Air Fryer Oven are crucial to ensuring its longevity and optimal performance. Follow this comprehensive guide to keep your appliance in top shape and ensure it continues to deliver delicious meals with ease.

Daily Cleaning

1. **Unplug and Cool Down**
    - Always unplug the air fryer oven and let it cool down completely before cleaning to avoid the risk of burns or electrical hazards.
2. **Remove Accessories**
    - Take out all removable parts, including the air fryer basket, crisper plate, baking tray, and any racks or pans you've used.
3. **Wash Removable Parts**
    - Wash these parts with warm, soapy water. Use a non-abrasive sponge or cloth to avoid scratching the non-stick surfaces. For tougher residues, let the items soak for a few minutes before scrubbing.
    - Alternatively, many of these parts are dishwasher-safe. Check the user manual to confirm which items can go in the dishwasher.
4. **Clean the Interior**
    - Wipe the oven's interior with a damp, non-abrasive cloth or sponge. Avoid using harsh chemicals or abrasive materials that can damage the interior surfaces.
    - For stubborn stains, mix baking soda and water to create a paste. Apply the paste to the stains, let it sit for a few minutes, and gently scrub with a non-abrasive sponge.
5. **Clean the Heating Element**
    - Check the heating element for any food debris or grease. Wipe it carefully with a damp cloth, being gentle to avoid damaging the element.
6. **Clean the Door**
    - Clean the door with a damp cloth, focusing on the glass window to ensure clear visibility. For grease buildup, use a small amount of dish soap diluted in water.
7. **Dry Thoroughly**
    - Make sure all parts and surfaces are thoroughly dry before reassembling the oven. This helps prevent mold and mildew growth and ensures safety during the subsequent use.

Weekly Cleaning

1. **Deep Clean Removable Parts**
    - Once a week, give the removable parts a more thorough cleaning. Soak them in warm, soapy water and use a soft brush to remove any built-up residue.
2. **Exterior Cleaning**
    - Wipe down the exterior of the air fryer oven with a damp cloth. Pay special attention to the control panel and handle, which can accumulate fingerprints and grease.

3. **Inspect for Wear and Tear**
    - Regularly inspect the accessories and interior for signs of wear and tear. Replace any parts that show significant damage to maintain the appliance's performance and safety.

Monthly Maintenance

1. **Check Air Vents**
    - Inspect the air vents on the back and sides of the unit to ensure they are free from dust and debris. Clean the vents with a soft brush or vacuum attachment to ensure proper air circulation and prevent overheating.
2. **Clean Fan**
    - If your model allows, check the fan for dust and debris. A clean fan ensures efficient air circulation and consistent cooking results.
3. **Descale the Oven**
    - If you notice mineral deposits or scale buildup, particularly if you use your oven frequently for steaming or with high-moisture foods, use a descaling solution recommended by the manufacturer or a mixture of vinegar and water. Follow the manufacturer's instructions for the descaling process.

Tips for Maintenance

1. **Avoid Harsh Chemicals**
    - Never use harsh chemicals, bleach, or abrasive cleaning tools on any part of your Ninja Foodi Digital Air Fryer Oven. These can damage the surfaces and affect the appliance's performance.
2. **Use Parchment Paper or Liners**
    - To minimize mess and make cleaning easier, use parchment paper or liners in the air fryer basket and baking trays. Ensure they are suitable for air fryers and won't block airflow.
3. **Regular Inspections**
    - Periodically check the power cord and plug for any signs of damage. If you notice any fraying or other issues, stop using the appliance and contact the manufacturer for repair or replacement.
4. **Store Properly**
    - Store your Ninja Foodi in a clean, dry place when not in use. Ensure all parts are dry before storing to prevent mold and mildew.

By following this maintenance and cleaning guide, you can keep your Ninja Foodi Digital Air Fryer Oven in excellent condition, ensuring it continues providing delicious, healthy meals for years. Regular care not only extends the life of your appliance but also ensures safe and efficient operation.

Chapter 1: Breakfast

Cinnamon French Toast Sticks

Time to Prepare: 10 minutes
Cooking Time: 8 minutes
Number of Servings: 4

Ingredients:

- 4 slices of thick-cut bread
- 2 large eggs
- 1/2 cup of milk
- 1 teaspoon of vanilla extract
- 1 teaspoon of ground cinnamon
- 1/4 cup of granulated sugar
- Non-stick cooking spray

Instructions List:

1. Preheat your Ninja Foodi Digital Air Fryer Oven to 360°F.
2. Cut each slice of bread into 3 or 4 sticks.
3. In a shallow bowl, whisk together the eggs, milk, and vanilla extract.
4. In another bowl, mix together the ground cinnamon and granulated sugar.
5. Dip each bread stick into the egg mixture, allowing any excess to drip off.
6. Lightly spray the air fryer basket with non-stick cooking spray.
7. Arrange the bread sticks in a single layer in the air fryer basket.
8. Air fry for 8 minutes, flipping halfway through, until golden and crispy.
9. Remove the French toast sticks from the air fryer and immediately roll them in the cinnamon-sugar mixture.
10. Serve warm with your favorite dipping sauce or syrup.

Nutritional Information (per serving):

- Calories: 210
- Protein: 6g
- Total Fats: 8g
- Fiber: 2g
- Carbohydrates: 29g

Breakfast Egg Muffins

Time to Prepare: 10 minutes
Cooking Time: 15 minutes
Number of Servings: 6

Ingredients:

- 6 large eggs
- 1/4 cup of milk
- 1 cup of diced bell peppers
- 1 cup of diced tomatoes
- 1 cup of chopped spinach
- 1/2 cup of shredded cheddar cheese
- Salt and pepper, to taste
- Non-stick cooking spray

Instructions List:

1. Preheat your Ninja Foodi Digital Air Fryer Oven to 350°F.
2. In a mixing bowl, whisk together the eggs and milk until well fat
3. Stir in the diced bell peppers, tomatoes, chopped spinach, and shredded cheddar cheese.
4. Season the mixture with salt and pepper to taste.
5. Lightly coat a muffin tin with non-stick cooking spray.
6. Evenly distribute the egg mixture into the muffin cups, filling each about 3/4 full.
7. Place the muffin tin in the air fryer basket.
8. Bake for 15 minutes or until the egg muffins are set and lightly golden on top.
9. Remove the muffin tin from the air fryer and let the egg muffins cool for a few minutes before serving.

Nutritional Information (per serving):

- Calories: 120
- Protein: 9g
- Total Fats: 8g
- Fiber: 1g
- Carbohydrates: 3g

Avocado Toast

Time to Prepare: 5 minutes
Cooking Time: 5 minutes
Number of Servings: 2

Ingredients:

- 1 ripe avocado
- 2 slices of bread (your choice)
- 1 tablespoon olive oil
- Salt and pepper, to taste
- Optional toppings: cherry tomatoes, red pepper flakes, fresh herbs

Instructions List:

1. Preheat your Ninja Foodi Digital Air Fryer Oven to 350°F.
2. Cut the avocado in half and remove the pit. Scoop out the avocado flesh into a bowl and mash it with a fork.
3. Drizzle olive oil over the avocado mash and season with salt and pepper to taste. Mix well.
4. Place the slices of bread on a baking tray lined with parchment paper.
5. Spread the avocado mixture evenly over each slice of bread.
6. Place the baking tray in the air fryer basket.
7. Air fry for 5 minutes or until the bread is toasted to your desired level of crispiness.
8. Remove the avocado toast from the air fryer and top with your favorite toppings, if desired.
9. Serve immediately.

Nutritional Information (per serving):

- Calories: 240
- Protein: 4g
- Total Fats: 16g
- Fiber: 6g
- Carbohydrates: 22g

Banana Pancake Bites

Time to Prepare: 10 minutes
Cooking Time: 10 minutes
Number of Servings: 4

Ingredients:

- 2 ripe bananas
- 2 large eggs
- 1/4 cup of milk (dairy or plant-based)
- 1 cup of rolled oats
- 1 teaspoon of vanilla extract
- 1/2 teaspoon of ground cinnamon
- Pinch of salt
- Maple syrup, for serving (optional)
- Fresh berries, for serving (optional)

Instructions List:

1. Preheat your Ninja Foodi Digital Air Fryer Oven to 350°F.
2. In a mixing bowl, mash the ripe bananas with a fork until smooth.
3. Add the eggs, milk, rolled oats, vanilla extract, ground cinnamon, and a pinch of salt to the bowl. Stir until well fat.
4. Lightly grease a mini muffin tin with non-stick cooking spray.
5. Pour the pancake batter into the mini muffin cups, filling each about 3/4 full.
6. Place the muffin tin in the air fryer basket.
7. Bake for 10 minutes or until the pancake bites are set and lightly golden on top.
8. Remove the muffin tin from the air fryer and let the pancake bites cool for a few minutes before serving.

9. Serve warm with maple syrup and fresh berries, if desired.

Nutritional Information (per serving):

- Calories: 180
- Protein: 6g
- Total Fats: 4g
- Fiber: 3g
- Carbohydrates: 32g

Crispy Hash Brown Patties

Time to Prepare: 10 minutes
Cooking Time: 15 minutes
Number of Servings: 4

Ingredients:

- 2 large russet potatoes, peeled and grated
- 1 small onion, grated
- 2 tablespoons all-purpose flour
- 1 teaspoon of salt
- 1/2 teaspoon of black pepper
- 1/2 teaspoon of garlic powder
- Non-stick cooking spray

Instructions List:

1. Preheat your Ninja Foodi Digital Air Fryer Oven to 375°F.
2. Place the grated potatoes and grated onion in a clean kitchen towel and squeeze out any excess moisture.
3. Transfer the dried potatoes and onion to a mixing bowl. Add the all-purpose flour, salt, black pepper, and garlic powder. Mix until well fat.
4. Divide the potato mixture into 8 equal portions and shape each portion into a flat, round patty.
5. Lightly grease the air fryer basket with non-stick cooking spray.
6. Arrange the hash brown patties in a single layer in the air fryer basket, making sure they are not touching.
7. Air fry for 15 minutes, flipping halfway through, or until the patties are golden brown and crispy on both sides.
8. Remove the hash brown patties from the air fryer and serve hot.

Nutritional Information (per serving):

- Calories: 110
- Protein: 2g
- Total Fats: 0.5g
- Fiber: 2g
- Carbohydrates: 25g

Apple Cinnamon Oatmeal Cups

Time to Prepare: 10 minutes
Cooking Time: 20 minutes
Number of Servings: 6

Ingredients:

- 2 cups of old-fashioned oats
- 1 teaspoon of ground cinnamon
- 1/4 teaspoon of ground nutmeg
- 1/4 teaspoon of salt
- 1 large apple, peeled and diced
- 1/4 cup of maple syrup
- 1 1/2 cups of milk (dairy or plant-based)
- 1 large egg
- 1 teaspoon of vanilla extract

Instructions List:

1. Preheat your Ninja Foodi Digital Air Fryer Oven to 350°F.
2. In a mixing bowl, combine the old-fashioned oats, ground cinnamon, ground nutmeg, and salt.
3. Add the diced apple to the bowl and mix until evenly distributed.
4. In a separate bowl, whisk together the maple syrup, milk, egg, and vanilla extract.
5. Pour the wet ingredients into the bowl with the dry ingredients and stir until well fat.

6. Lightly grease a muffin tin with non-stick cooking spray or line with silicone muffin liners.
7. Divide the oatmeal mixture evenly among the muffin cups, filling each about 3/4 full.
8. Place the muffin tin in the air fryer basket.
9. Bake for 20 minutes or until the oatmeal cups are set and lightly golden on top.
10. Remove the muffin tin from the air fryer and let the oatmeal cups cool for a few minutes before serving.

Nutritional Information (per serving):

- Calories: 180
- Protein: 6g
- Total Fats: 3g
- Fiber: 3g
- Carbohydrates: 32g

Breakfast Burritos

Time to Prepare: 15 minutes
Cooking Time: 10 minutes
Number of Servings: 4

Ingredients:

- 4 large flour tortillas
- 4 large eggs
- 1/4 cup of milk
- 1 cup of cooked breakfast sausage, crumbled
- 1/2 cup of shredded cheddar cheese
- 1/2 cup of diced bell peppers
- 1/4 cup of diced onion
- Salt and pepper, to taste
- Non-stick cooking spray

Instructions List:

1. Preheat your Ninja Foodi Digital Air Fryer Oven to 375°F.
2. In a mixing bowl, whisk together the eggs and milk until well fat. Season with salt and pepper to taste.
3. Heat a skillet over medium heat and lightly spray with non-stick cooking spray.
4. Pour the egg mixture into the skillet and scramble until cooked through. Remove from heat.
5. Lay out the flour tortillas on a clean surface.
6. Divide the scrambled eggs, cooked breakfast sausage, shredded cheddar cheese, diced bell peppers, and diced onion evenly among the tortillas, placing the fillings in the center of each tortilla.
7. Fold the sides of each tortilla over the filling, then roll up tightly to form burritos.
8. Lightly spray the air fryer basket with non-stick cooking spray.
9. Place the burritos seam-side down in the air fryer basket, making sure they are not touching.
10. Air fry for 10 minutes or until the burritos are golden and crispy on the outside.
11. Remove the breakfast burritos from the air fryer and serve hot.

Nutritional Information (per serving):

- Calories: 320
- Protein: 18g
- Total Fats: 16g
- Fiber: 2g
- Carbohydrates: 25g

Blueberry Breakfast Scones

Time to Prepare: 15 minutes
Cooking Time: 15 minutes
Number of Servings: 8

Ingredients:

- 2 cups of all-purpose flour
- 1/4 cup of granulated sugar
- 1 tablespoon baking powder
- 1/2 teaspoon of salt
- 1/2 cup of cold unsalted butter, cubed

- 1/2 cup of milk (dairy or plant-based)
- 1 large egg
- 1 teaspoon of vanilla extract
- 1 cup of fresh or frozen blueberries

Instructions List:

1. Preheat your Ninja Foodi Digital Air Fryer Oven to 375°F.
2. In a large mixing bowl, whisk together the all-purpose flour, granulated sugar, baking powder, and salt.
3. Add the cold cubed butter to the bowl and use a pastry cutter or fork to cut the butter into the dry ingredients until the mixture resembles coarse crumbs.
4. In a separate small bowl, whisk together the milk, egg, and vanilla extract.
5. Pour the wet ingredients into the bowl with the dry ingredients and mix until just fat.
6. Gently fold in the blueberries until evenly distributed throughout the dough.
7. Turn the dough out onto a lightly floured surface and pat it into a circle about 1 inch thick.
8. Use a sharp knife or bench scraper to cut the circle into 8 wedges.
9. Place the scones on a baking tray lined with parchment paper or a silicone baking mat.
10. Bake for 15 minutes or until the scones are lightly golden on top and cooked through.
11. Remove the scones from the air fryer and let them cool on a wire rack before serving.

Nutritional Information (per serving):

- Calories: 240
- Protein: 4g
- Total Fats: 11g
- Fiber: 1g
- Carbohydrates: 31g

Sweet Potato Breakfast Hash

Time to Prepare: 15 minutes
Cooking Time: 25 minutes
Number of Servings: 4

Ingredients:

- 2 large sweet potatoes, peeled and diced
- 1 bell pepper, diced
- 1 onion, diced
- 2 cloves garlic, minced
- 2 tablespoons olive oil
- 1 teaspoon of paprika
- 1/2 teaspoon of garlic powder
- 1/2 teaspoon of onion powder
- Salt and pepper, to taste
- 4 large eggs

Instructions List:

1. Preheat your Ninja Foodi Digital Air Fryer Oven to 375°F.
2. In a large mixing bowl, toss together the diced sweet potatoes, diced bell pepper, diced onion, minced garlic, olive oil, paprika, garlic powder, onion powder, salt, and pepper until evenly coated.
3. Spread the sweet potato mixture out in a single layer on a baking tray lined with parchment paper or a silicone baking mat.
4. Place the baking tray in the air fryer basket.
5. Roast for 25 minutes or until the sweet potatoes are tender and golden brown, stirring halfway through the cooking time.
6. Create 4 wells in the roasted sweet potato mixture and crack an egg into each well.
7. Return the baking tray to the air fryer basket.
8. Roast for an additional 8-10 minutes or until the egg whites are set but the yolks are still runny, or until cooked to your desired level of doneness.
9. Remove the sweet potato breakfast hash from the air fryer and serve hot.

Nutritional Information (per serving):

- Calories: 260
- Protein: 8g
- Total Fats: 12g
- Fiber: 5g
- Carbohydrates: 30g

Spinach and Feta Stuffed Croissants

Time to Prepare: 15 minutes
Cooking Time: 12 minutes
Number of Servings: 4

Ingredients:

- 1 sheet of puff pastry, thawed
- 1 cup of fresh spinach leaves
- 1/2 cup of crumbled feta cheese
- 1/4 cup of diced sun-dried tomatoes
- 1 clove garlic, minced
- 1 tablespoon olive oil
- Salt and pepper, to taste
- 1 large egg, beaten (for egg wash)

Instructions List:

1. Preheat your Ninja Foodi Digital Air Fryer Oven to 375°F.
2. In a skillet over medium heat, heat the olive oil. Add the minced garlic and sauté until fragrant.
3. Add the fresh spinach leaves to the skillet and cook until wilted. Season with salt and pepper to taste.
4. Remove the skillet from heat and transfer the cooked spinach to a mixing bowl. Let it cool slightly.
5. Stir in the crumbled feta cheese and diced sun-dried tomatoes into the spinach mixture until well fat.
6. Unroll the thawed puff pastry sheet onto a clean surface.
7. Cut the puff pastry into 4 equal squares.
8. Divide the spinach and feta mixture evenly among the puff pastry squares, placing it in the center of each square.
9. Fold the corners of each puff pastry square over the filling, forming a triangle shape.
10. Press the edges of the puff pastry together to seal the filling inside.
11. Place the stuffed croissants on a baking tray lined with parchment paper.
12. Brush the tops of the croissants with the beaten egg to create a golden crust.
13. Place the baking tray in the air fryer basket.
14. Bake for 12 minutes or until the stuffed croissants are puffed up and golden brown.
15. Remove the baking tray from the air fryer and let the croissants cool for a few minutes before serving.

Nutritional Information (per serving):

- Calories: 280
- Protein: 7g
- Total Fats: 18g
- Fiber: 2g
- Carbohydrates: 23g

Churro Donuts

Time to Prepare: 15 minutes
Cooking Time: 10 minutes
Number of Servings: 6

Ingredients:

- 1 can (8-count) refrigerated biscuit dough
- 1/4 cup of granulated sugar
- 1 tablespoon ground cinnamon
- 2 tablespoons unsalted butter, melted

Instructions List:

1. Preheat your Ninja Foodi Digital Air Fryer Oven to 350°F.
2. Open the can of refrigerated biscuit dough and separate the biscuits.

3. Using your thumb or a small round object, make a hole in the center of each biscuit to form a donut shape.
4. In a shallow bowl, mix together the granulated sugar and ground cinnamon.
5. Lightly brush each biscuit with melted butter, then coat them generously in the cinnamon-sugar mixture.
6. Arrange the coated biscuit donuts in a single layer in the air fryer basket, making sure they are not touching.
7. Air fry for 10 minutes or until the donuts are golden brown and cooked through.
8. Remove the donuts from the air fryer and let them cool for a few minutes before serving.

Nutritional Information (per serving):

- Calories: 200
- Protein: 3g
- Total Fats: 10g
- Fiber: 1g
- Carbohydrates: 25g

Lemon Poppy Seed Muffins

Time to Prepare: 10 minutes
Cooking Time: 20 minutes
Number of Servings: 12

Ingredients:

- 2 cups of all-purpose flour
- 1/2 cup of granulated sugar
- 2 teaspoons of baking powder
- 1/2 teaspoon of baking soda
- 1/4 teaspoon of salt
- Zest of 1 lemon
- 1/4 cup of fresh lemon juice
- 1/2 cup of unsalted butter, melted and cooled
- 1/2 cup of Greek yogurt
- 2 large eggs
- 1 teaspoon of vanilla extract
- 1 tablespoon poppy seeds

Instructions List:

1. Preheat your Ninja Foodi Digital Air Fryer Oven to 350°F.
2. In a large mixing bowl, whisk together the all-purpose flour, granulated sugar, baking powder, baking soda, salt, and lemon zest.
3. In a separate bowl, mix together the fresh lemon juice, melted butter, Greek yogurt, eggs, and vanilla extract until well fat.
4. Pour the wet ingredients into the bowl with the dry ingredients and stir until just fat. Be careful not to overmix.
5. Gently fold in the poppy seeds until evenly distributed throughout the batter.
6. Line a muffin tin with paper liners or lightly grease the muffin cups with non-stick cooking spray.
7. Divide the batter evenly among the muffin cups, filling each about 3/4 full.
8. Place the muffin tin in the air fryer basket.
9. Bake for 20 minutes or until a toothpick inserted into the center of a muffin comes out clean.
10. Remove the muffin tin from the air fryer and let the muffins cool in the tin for a few minutes before transferring them to a wire rack to cool completely.

Nutritional Information (per serving):

- Calories: 190
- Protein: 4g
- Total Fats: 9g
- Fiber: 1g
- Carbohydrates: 24g

Breakfast Quesadillas

Time to Prepare: 10 minutes
Cooking Time: 8 minutes
Number of Servings: 2

Ingredients:

- 4 small flour tortillas
- 4 large eggs
- 1/4 cup of milk (dairy or plant-based)
- 1/2 cup of shredded cheddar cheese
- 1/2 cup of cooked breakfast sausage, crumbled
- 1/4 cup of diced bell peppers
- 1/4 cup of diced onion
- Salt and pepper, to taste
- Non-stick cooking spray

Instructions List:

1. Preheat your Ninja Foodi Digital Air Fryer Oven to 375°F.
2. In a mixing bowl, whisk together the eggs and milk until well fat. Season with salt and pepper to taste.
3. Heat a skillet over medium heat and lightly spray with non-stick cooking spray.
4. Pour the egg mixture into the skillet and scramble until cooked through. Remove from heat.
5. Lay out 2 flour tortillas on a clean surface.
6. Divide the scrambled eggs, shredded cheddar cheese, cooked breakfast sausage, diced bell peppers, and diced onion evenly between the tortillas, placing the fillings on one half of each tortilla.
7. Fold the other half of each tortilla over the filling to form a half-moon shape.
8. Lightly spray the air fryer basket with non-stick cooking spray.
9. Place the quesadillas in the air fryer basket.
10. Air fry for 4 minutes, then carefully flip the quesadillas and air fry for an additional 4 minutes or until crispy and golden brown.
11. Remove the breakfast quesadillas from the air fryer and let them cool for a few minutes before serving.

Nutritional Information (per serving):

- Calories: 420
- Protein: 22g
- Total Fats: 25g
- Fiber: 2g
- Carbohydrates: 28g

Almond Butter Banana Toast

Time to Prepare: 5 minutes
Cooking Time: 5 minutes
Number of Servings: 2

Ingredients:

- 2 slices whole wheat bread
- 2 tablespoons almond butter
- 1 ripe banana, thinly sliced
- 1 tablespoon honey (optional)
- Pinch of cinnamon (optional)

Instructions List:

1. Preheat your Ninja Foodi Digital Air Fryer Oven to 350°F.
2. Place the slices of whole wheat bread on a clean surface.
3. Spread 1 tablespoon of almond butter evenly onto each slice of bread.
4. Arrange the thinly sliced banana on top of the almond butter layer.
5. Drizzle with honey and sprinkle with cinnamon, if desired.
6. Place the prepared toast in the air fryer basket.
7. Air fry for 5 minutes or until the bread is toasted and the bananas are slightly caramelized.
8. Remove the almond butter banana toast from the air fryer and serve warm.

Nutritional Information (per serving):

- Calories: 260
- Protein: 6g
- Total Fats: 12g
- Fiber: 5g

- Carbohydrates: 35g

Chapter 2: Poultry

Garlic Parmesan Chicken Wings

Time to Prepare: 10 minutes
Cooking Time: 20 minutes
Number of Servings: 4

Ingredients:

- 2 lbs chicken wings, split at joints, tips removed
- 2 tablespoons olive oil
- 4 cloves garlic, minced
- 1/4 cup of grated Parmesan cheese
- 1 teaspoon of dried oregano
- 1/2 teaspoon of dried basil
- 1/2 teaspoon of dried thyme
- Salt and pepper, to taste
- Chopped fresh parsley, for garnish (optional)

Instructions List:

1. Preheat your Ninja Foodi Digital Air Fryer Oven to 380°F.
2. In a large mixing bowl, toss the chicken wings with olive oil, minced garlic, grated Parmesan cheese, dried oregano, dried basil, dried thyme, salt, and pepper until evenly coated.
3. Place the seasoned chicken wings in the air fryer basket, making sure they are in a single layer and not overcrowded.
4. Air fry for 10 minutes, then flip the chicken wings using tongs.
5. Continue to air fry for an additional 10 minutes or until the chicken wings are golden brown and crispy.
6. Remove the chicken wings from the air fryer and transfer them to a serving platter.
7. Garnish with chopped fresh parsley, if desired, before serving.

Nutritional Information (per serving):

- Calories: 370
- Protein: 26g
- Total Fats: 27g
- Fiber: 1g
- Carbohydrates: 2g

Chicken Tenders

Time to Prepare: 15 minutes
Cooking Time: 12 minutes
Number of Servings: 4

Ingredients:

- 1 lb chicken tenders
- 1 cup of breadcrumbs
- 1/2 cup of grated Parmesan cheese
- 1 teaspoon of garlic powder
- 1 teaspoon of paprika
- 1/2 teaspoon of salt
- 1/4 teaspoon of black pepper
- 2 large eggs
- Non-stick cooking spray

Instructions List:

1. Preheat your Ninja Foodi Digital Air Fryer Oven to 400°F.
2. In a shallow dish, mix together the breadcrumbs, grated Parmesan cheese, garlic powder, paprika, salt, and black pepper.
3. In another shallow dish, beat the eggs.
4. Dip each chicken tender into the beaten eggs, then coat it evenly with the breadcrumb mixture.
5. Place the coated chicken tenders in a single layer on the air fryer basket, making sure they are not touching.
6. Lightly spray the chicken tenders with non-stick cooking spray.
7. Air fry for 6 minutes, then flip the chicken tenders using tongs.

8. Continue to air fry for an additional 6 minutes or until the chicken tenders are golden brown and cooked through.
9. Remove the chicken tenders from the air fryer and let them cool for a few minutes before serving.

Nutritional Information (per serving):

- Calories: 280
- Protein: 30g
- Total Fats: 11g
- Fiber: 1g
- Carbohydrates: 14g

Buffalo Chicken Drumsticks

Time to Prepare: 10 minutes
Cooking Time: 25 minutes
Number of Servings: 4

Ingredients:

- 8 chicken drumsticks
- 1/4 cup of hot sauce (such as Frank's RedHot)
- 2 tablespoons unsalted butter, melted
- 1 tablespoon white vinegar
- 1/2 teaspoon of garlic powder
- 1/2 teaspoon of onion powder
- Salt and pepper, to taste
- Ranch or blue cheese dressing, for serving (optional)
- Celery sticks, for serving (optional)

Instructions List:

1. Preheat your Ninja Foodi Digital Air Fryer Oven to 400°F.
2. In a small bowl, whisk together the hot sauce, melted butter, white vinegar, garlic powder, onion powder, salt, and pepper until well fat.
3. Pat the chicken drumsticks dry with paper towels.
4. Place the chicken drumsticks in a large mixing bowl and pour the buffalo sauce mixture over them, tossing to coat evenly.
5. Arrange the coated chicken drumsticks in a single layer in the air fryer basket.
6. Air fry for 20 minutes, flipping the drumsticks halfway through the cooking time.
7. Air fry for an additional 5 minutes or until the chicken drumsticks are cooked through and crispy.
8. Remove the chicken drumsticks from the air fryer and let them rest for a few minutes before serving.
9. Serve with ranch or blue cheese dressing and celery sticks, if desired.

Nutritional Information (per serving):

- Calories: 320
- Protein: 24g
- Total Fats: 18g
- Fiber: 0g
- Carbohydrates: 4g

Lemon Herb Roast Chicken

Time to Prepare: 15 minutes
Cooking Time: 45 minutes
Number of Servings: 4

Ingredients:

- 1 whole chicken (about 4 lbs), giblets removed
- 2 tablespoons olive oil
- Zest and juice of 1 lemon
- 2 cloves garlic, minced
- 1 tablespoon chopped fresh thyme
- 1 tablespoon chopped fresh rosemary
- 1 tablespoon chopped fresh parsley
- Salt and pepper, to taste
- Lemon slices, for garnish (optional)

Instructions List:

1. Preheat your Ninja Foodi Digital Air Fryer Oven to 375°F.
2. In a small bowl, mix together the olive oil, lemon zest, lemon juice, minced garlic, chopped fresh thyme, chopped fresh rosemary, chopped fresh parsley, salt, and pepper to create a marinade.
3. Place the whole chicken in a large mixing bowl and rub the marinade all over the chicken, making sure it is well coated inside and out.
4. Tie the legs of the chicken together with kitchen twine, if desired.
5. Place the chicken breast-side up in the air fryer basket.
6. Roast for 45 minutes or until the chicken is cooked through and the skin is golden brown, basting with any remaining marinade halfway through the cooking time.
7. Insert a meat thermometer into the thickest part of the chicken to ensure it has reached an internal temperature of 165°F.
8. Once cooked, remove the chicken from the air fryer and let it rest for 10 minutes before carving.
9. Garnish with lemon slices, if desired, before serving.

Nutritional Information (per serving):

- Calories: 360
- Protein: 30g
- Total Fats: 22g
- Fiber: 1g
- Carbohydrates: 2g

Chicken Parmesan

Time to Prepare: 15 minutes
Cooking Time: 20 minutes
Number of Servings: 4

Ingredients:

- 4 boneless, skinless chicken breasts
- 1/2 cup of breadcrumbs
- 1/4 cup of grated Parmesan cheese
- 1 teaspoon of Italian seasoning
- 1/2 teaspoon of garlic powder
- 1/2 teaspoon of onion powder
- Salt and pepper, to taste
- 1 cup of marinara sauce
- 1 cup of shredded mozzarella cheese
- Fresh basil leaves, for garnish (optional)

Instructions List:

1. Preheat your Ninja Foodi Digital Air Fryer Oven to 375°F.
2. In a shallow dish, mix together the breadcrumbs, grated Parmesan cheese, Italian seasoning, garlic powder, onion powder, salt, and pepper.
3. Pat the chicken breasts dry with paper towels.
4. Coat each chicken breast evenly with the breadcrumb mixture, pressing lightly to adhere.
5. Place the coated chicken breasts in a single layer in the air fryer basket.
6. Air fry for 10 minutes, then flip the chicken breasts using tongs.
7. Spoon marinara sauce over each chicken breast and sprinkle with shredded mozzarella cheese.
8. Air fry for an additional 10 minutes or until the chicken is cooked through and the cheese is melted and bubbly.
9. Remove the chicken Parmesan from the air fryer and let it rest for a few minutes before serving.
10. Garnish with fresh basil leaves, if desired, before serving.

Nutritional Information (per serving):

- Calories: 320
- Protein: 35g
- Total Fats: 10g
- Fiber: 2g

- Carbohydrates: 20g

Spicy Sriracha Chicken Bites

Time to Prepare: 15 minutes
Cooking Time: 15 minutes
Number of Servings: 4

Ingredients:

- 1 lb boneless, skinless chicken breasts, cut into bite-sized pieces
- 1/4 cup of sriracha sauce
- 2 tablespoons honey
- 1 tablespoon soy sauce
- 1 tablespoon rice vinegar
- 1 teaspoon of sesame oil
- 1 teaspoon of minced garlic
- 1/2 teaspoon of grated ginger
- 1 tablespoon cornstarch
- Sesame seeds, for garnish (optional)
- Sliced green onions, for garnish (optional)

Instructions List:

1. Preheat your Ninja Foodi Digital Air Fryer Oven to 375°F.
2. In a mixing bowl, whisk together the sriracha sauce, honey, soy sauce, rice vinegar, sesame oil, minced garlic, grated ginger, and cornstarch until well fat.
3. Add the chicken breast pieces to the bowl and toss to coat evenly with the sauce mixture.
4. Place the coated chicken pieces in a single layer in the air fryer basket, making sure they are not touching.
5. Air fry for 15 minutes or until the chicken is cooked through and crispy, shaking the basket halfway through the cooking time.
6. Remove the chicken bites from the air fryer and let them cool for a few minutes before serving.
7. Garnish with sesame seeds and sliced green onions, if desired, before serving.

Nutritional Information (per serving):

- Calories: 280
- Protein: 25g
- Total Fats: 5g
- Fiber: 1g
- Carbohydrates: 30g

Teriyaki Chicken Skewers

Time to Prepare: 20 minutes
Cooking Time: 15 minutes
Number of Servings: 4

Ingredients:

- 1 lb boneless, skinless chicken breasts, cut into cubes
- 1/4 cup of soy sauce
- 2 tablespoons honey
- 1 tablespoon rice vinegar
- 1 teaspoon of sesame oil
- 1 teaspoon of minced garlic
- 1/2 teaspoon of grated ginger
- 1 tablespoon cornstarch
- Bamboo skewers, soaked in water for 30 minutes
- Sesame seeds, for garnish (optional)
- Sliced green onions, for garnish (optional)

Instructions List:

1. Preheat your Ninja Foodi Digital Air Fryer Oven to 375°F.
2. In a mixing bowl, whisk together the soy sauce, honey, rice vinegar, sesame oil, minced garlic, grated ginger, and cornstarch until well fat.
3. Add the chicken cubes to the bowl and toss to coat evenly with the sauce mixture. Allow the chicken to marinate for at least 10 minutes.
4. Thread the marinated chicken cubes onto the soaked bamboo skewers.

5. Place the chicken skewers in a single layer in the air fryer basket, making sure they are not touching.
6. Air fry for 15 minutes or until the chicken is cooked through, turning the skewers halfway through the cooking time.
7. Remove the chicken skewers from the air fryer and let them cool for a few minutes before serving.
8. Garnish with sesame seeds and sliced green onions, if desired, before serving.

Nutritional Information (per serving):

- Calories: 240
- Protein: 25g
- Total Fats: 5g
- Fiber: 1g
- Carbohydrates: 20g

Crispy Buttermilk Chicken Breasts

Time to Prepare: 10 minutes
Cooking Time: 20 minutes
Number of Servings: 4

Ingredients:

- 4 boneless, skinless chicken breasts
- 1 cup of buttermilk
- 1 cup of breadcrumbs
- 1/4 cup of grated Parmesan cheese
- 1 teaspoon of paprika
- 1 teaspoon of garlic powder
- 1 teaspoon of onion powder
- Salt and pepper, to taste
- Non-stick cooking spray

Instructions List:

1. Preheat your Ninja Foodi Digital Air Fryer Oven to 375°F.
2. Place the chicken breasts in a shallow dish and pour the buttermilk over them. Let them marinate for at least 30 minutes.
3. In another shallow dish, mix together the breadcrumbs, grated Parmesan cheese, paprika, garlic powder, onion powder, salt, and pepper.
4. Remove the chicken breasts from the buttermilk, allowing any excess to drip off.
5. Coat each chicken breast evenly with the breadcrumb mixture, pressing lightly to adhere.
6. Place the coated chicken breasts in a single layer in the air fryer basket, making sure they are not touching.
7. Lightly spray the chicken breasts with non-stick cooking spray.
8. Air fry for 20 minutes or until the chicken is cooked through and golden brown, flipping halfway through the cooking time.
9. Remove the chicken breasts from the air fryer and let them rest for a few minutes before serving.

Nutritional Information (per serving):

- Calories: 320
- Protein: 30g
- Total Fats: 10g
- Fiber: 1g
- Carbohydrates: 20g

Mediterranean Stuffed Chicken

Time to Prepare: 20 minutes
Cooking Time: 25 minutes
Number of Servings: 4

Ingredients:

- 4 boneless, skinless chicken breasts
- 1/2 cup of sun-dried tomatoes, chopped
- 1/4 cup of Kalamata olives, chopped
- 1/4 cup of crumbled feta cheese
- 2 tablespoons chopped fresh basil

- 1 tablespoon chopped fresh oregano
- 1 tablespoon olive oil
- 1 teaspoon of minced garlic
- Salt and pepper, to taste
- Toothpicks

Instructions List:

1. Preheat your Ninja Foodi Digital Air Fryer Oven to 375°F.
2. In a mixing bowl, combine the sun-dried tomatoes, Kalamata olives, crumbled feta cheese, chopped fresh basil, chopped fresh oregano, olive oil, minced garlic, salt, and pepper.
3. Lay the chicken breasts flat on a clean surface and use a sharp knife to cut a pocket horizontally into each chicken breast.
4. Stuff each chicken breast with the Mediterranean mixture, dividing it evenly among the chicken breasts.
5. Secure the pockets closed with toothpicks.
6. Place the stuffed chicken breasts in a single layer in the air fryer basket.
7. Bake for 25 minutes or until the chicken is cooked through and the filling is heated through.
8. Remove the stuffed chicken breasts from the air fryer and let them rest for a few minutes before serving.

Nutritional Information (per serving):

- Calories: 280
- Protein: 35g
- Total Fats: 12g
- Fiber: 3g
- Carbohydrates: 5g

BBQ Chicken Pizza

Time to Prepare: 15 minutes
Cooking Time: 15 minutes
Number of Servings: 4

Ingredients:

- 1 pre-made pizza dough
- 1/2 cup of BBQ sauce
- 1 cup of cooked chicken breast, shredded
- 1/2 cup of red onion, thinly sliced
- 1 cup of shredded mozzarella cheese
- 1/4 cup of chopped fresh cilantro
- Olive oil, for brushing

Instructions List:

1. Preheat your Ninja Foodi Digital Air Fryer Oven to 375°F.
2. Roll out the pizza dough on a lightly floured surface to fit the size of your air fryer basket.
3. Transfer the rolled-out dough to a piece of parchment paper.
4. Spread the BBQ sauce evenly over the pizza dough, leaving a small border around the edges.
5. Sprinkle the shredded chicken breast and sliced red onion over the BBQ sauce.
6. Top with shredded mozzarella cheese.
7. Carefully transfer the pizza on the parchment paper to the air fryer basket.
8. Bake for 15 minutes or until the crust is golden brown and the cheese is melted and bubbly.
9. Remove the pizza from the air fryer and let it cool for a few minutes before slicing.
10. Garnish with chopped fresh cilantro before serving.

Nutritional Information (per serving):

- Calories: 340
- Protein: 20g
- Total Fats: 10g
- Fiber: 2g
- Carbohydrates: 45g

Chicken and Vegetable Stir-Fry

Time to Prepare: 15 minutes
Cooking Time: 15 minutes
Number of Servings: 4

Ingredients:

- 1 lb boneless, skinless chicken breast, thinly sliced
- 2 cups of mixed vegetables (such as bell peppers, broccoli, snap peas, carrots)
- 2 tablespoons soy sauce
- 1 tablespoon hoisin sauce
- 1 tablespoon oyster sauce
- 1 teaspoon of sesame oil
- 1 teaspoon of minced garlic
- 1/2 teaspoon of grated ginger
- 2 tablespoons olive oil
- Cooked rice or noodles, for serving

Instructions List:

1. Preheat your Ninja Foodi Digital Air Fryer Oven to 400°F on the Broil setting.
2. In a small bowl, mix together the soy sauce, hoisin sauce, oyster sauce, sesame oil, minced garlic, and grated ginger to create the sauce.
3. Heat olive oil in a large skillet or wok over medium-high heat.
4. Add the sliced chicken breast to the skillet and stir-fry for 3-4 minutes or until cooked through.
5. Add the mixed vegetables to the skillet and continue to stir-fry for another 3-4 minutes or until the vegetables are tender-crisp.
6. Pour the sauce over the chicken and vegetables in the skillet and toss to coat evenly.
7. Transfer the chicken and vegetable stir-fry to a baking dish suitable for broiling in the air fryer.
8. Place the baking dish in the air fryer basket and broil for 5-6 minutes or until the sauce is bubbling and slightly thickened.
9. Serve the chicken and vegetable stir-fry hot over cooked rice or noodles.

Nutritional Information (per serving):

- Calories: 280
- Protein: 25g
- Total Fats: 12g
- Fiber: 4g
- Carbohydrates: 18g

Chicken Empanadas

Time to Prepare: 30 minutes
Cooking Time: 15 minutes
Number of Servings: 6

Ingredients:

- 1 lb cooked chicken breast, shredded
- 1/2 cup of diced onion
- 1/2 cup of diced bell pepper
- 1/2 cup of frozen corn kernels, thawed
- 1/2 cup of black beans, drained and rinsed
- 1/2 cup of shredded cheddar cheese
- 2 tablespoons chopped fresh cilantro
- 1 teaspoon of ground cumin
- 1/2 teaspoon of chili powder
- Salt and pepper, to taste
- 1 package refrigerated pie crusts (2 crusts)
- 1 egg, beaten (for egg wash)

Instructions List:

1. Preheat your Ninja Foodi Digital Air Fryer Oven to 375°F.
2. In a large mixing bowl, combine the shredded chicken breast, diced onion, diced bell pepper, thawed corn kernels, black beans, shredded cheddar cheese, chopped fresh cilantro, ground cumin, chili powder, salt, and pepper. Mix well to combine.
3. Unroll the refrigerated pie crusts on a lightly floured surface. Use a rolling pin to roll out the dough slightly thinner.

4. Use a round cookie cutter or a small bowl to cut circles out of the pie crusts.
5. Place a spoonful of the chicken mixture onto one half of each pie crust circle.
6. Fold the other half of the pie crust over the filling to form a half-moon shape. Press the edges together to seal, then crimp with a fork to secure.
7. Brush the tops of the empanadas with beaten egg for a golden finish.
8. Place the empanadas in a single layer in the air fryer basket, leaving space between each one.
9. Air fry for 12-15 minutes or until the empanadas are golden brown and crispy.
10. Remove the empanadas from the air fryer and let them cool for a few minutes before serving.

Nutritional Information (per serving):

- Calories: 320
- Protein: 20g
- Total Fats: 15g
- Fiber: 2g
- Carbohydrates: 25g

Thai Peanut Chicken Satay

Time to Prepare: 20 minutes
Cooking Time: 15 minutes
Number of Servings: 4

Ingredients:

- 1 lb chicken breast, cut into thin strips
- 1/4 cup of creamy peanut butter
- 2 tablespoons soy sauce
- 1 tablespoon honey
- 1 tablespoon lime juice
- 2 teaspoons of minced garlic
- 1 teaspoon of grated ginger
- 1/2 teaspoon of ground cumin
- 1/4 teaspoon of cayenne pepper
- Salt and pepper, to taste
- Bamboo skewers, soaked in water for 30 minutes
- Chopped peanuts and chopped fresh cilantro, for garnish (optional)

Instructions List:

1. Preheat your Ninja Foodi Digital Air Fryer Oven to 375°F.
2. In a mixing bowl, whisk together the peanut butter, soy sauce, honey, lime juice, minced garlic, grated ginger, ground cumin, cayenne pepper, salt, and pepper to create the marinade.
3. Add the chicken strips to the marinade and toss to coat evenly. Allow the chicken to marinate for at least 15 minutes.
4. Thread the marinated chicken strips onto the soaked bamboo skewers.
5. Place the chicken skewers in a single layer in the air fryer basket.
6. Air fry for 15 minutes or until the chicken is cooked through, turning the skewers halfway through the cooking time.
7. Remove the chicken satay from the air fryer and let them cool for a few minutes before serving.
8. Garnish with chopped peanuts and chopped fresh cilantro, if desired, before serving.

Nutritional Information (per serving):

- Calories: 280
- Protein: 25g
- Total Fats: 15g
- Fiber: 2g
- Carbohydrates: 10g

Chicken Taquitos

Time to Prepare: 20 minutes
Cooking Time: 15 minutes
Number of Servings: 4

Ingredients:

- 1 lb cooked chicken breast, shredded

- 1/2 cup of canned black beans, drained and rinsed
- 1/2 cup of corn kernels (fresh, canned, or frozen)
- 1/2 cup of shredded Mexican blend cheese
- 1/4 cup of chopped fresh cilantro
- 1 teaspoon of chili powder
- 1/2 teaspoon of ground cumin
- 1/2 teaspoon of garlic powder
- Salt and pepper, to taste
- 12 small corn tortillas
- Non-stick cooking spray

Instructions List:

1. Preheat your Ninja Foodi Digital Air Fryer Oven to 375°F.
2. In a large mixing bowl, combine the shredded chicken breast, black beans, corn kernels, shredded cheese, chopped cilantro, chili powder, ground cumin, garlic powder, salt, and pepper. Mix well to combine.
3. Warm the corn tortillas in the microwave for about 20-30 seconds to make them pliable.
4. Spoon a portion of the chicken mixture onto each corn tortilla, then roll tightly to form taquitos.
5. Place the rolled taquitos seam-side down in the air fryer basket, ensuring they are not touching each other.
6. Lightly spray the taquitos with non-stick cooking spray.
7. Air fry for 12-15 minutes or until the taquitos are golden and crispy.
8. Remove the taquitos from the air fryer and let them cool for a few minutes before serving.
9. Serve with your favorite dipping sauce, such as salsa, guacamole, or sour cream.

Nutritional Information (per serving):

- Calories: 280
- Protein: 25g
- Total Fats: 10g
- Fiber: 5g
- Carbohydrates: 20g

Chapter 3: Beef, Pork & Lamb

Meatballs

Time to Prepare: 15 minutes
Cooking Time: 15 minutes
Number of Servings: 4

Ingredients:

- 1 lb ground beef (or combination of beef and pork)
- 1/4 cup of breadcrumbs
- 1/4 cup of grated Parmesan cheese
- 1/4 cup of chopped fresh parsley
- 1 teaspoon of minced garlic
- 1/2 teaspoon of onion powder
- 1/2 teaspoon of dried oregano
- 1/2 teaspoon of dried basil
- 1/4 teaspoon of salt
- 1/4 teaspoon of black pepper
- 1 egg, lightly beaten
- Non-stick cooking spray

Instructions List:

1. Preheat your Ninja Foodi Digital Air Fryer Oven to 375°F.
2. In a large mixing bowl, combine the ground beef, breadcrumbs, grated Parmesan cheese, chopped parsley, minced garlic, onion powder, dried oregano, dried basil, salt, pepper, and beaten egg. Mix well until all ingredients are evenly incorporated.
3. Roll the meat mixture into small balls, about 1-inch in diameter, and place them on a plate.
4. Lightly spray the air fryer basket with non-stick cooking spray.
5. Arrange the meatballs in a single layer in the air fryer basket, leaving a little space between each one.
6. Air fry for 12-15 minutes, shaking the basket halfway through cooking, until the meatballs are browned and cooked through.
7. Once cooked, remove the meatballs from the air fryer and let them rest for a few minutes before serving.

Nutritional Information (per serving):

- Calories: 280
- Protein: 25g
- Total Fats: 18g
- Fiber: 1g
- Carbohydrates: 5g

BBQ Pork Ribs

Time to Prepare: 20 minutes
Cooking Time: 1 hour 30 minutes
Number of Servings: 4

Ingredients:

- 2 racks pork ribs
- 1 cup of BBQ sauce
- 2 tablespoons brown sugar
- 1 tablespoon Worcestershire sauce
- 1 tablespoon apple cider vinegar
- 1 teaspoon of smoked paprika
- 1/2 teaspoon of garlic powder
- 1/2 teaspoon of onion powder
- Salt and pepper, to taste

Instructions List:

1. Preheat your Ninja Foodi Digital Air Fryer Oven to 300°F on the Roast setting.
2. Remove the membrane from the back of the ribs, if present, then season the ribs generously with salt and pepper.
3. In a small bowl, mix together the BBQ sauce, brown sugar, Worcestershire sauce, apple cider vinegar, smoked paprika, garlic powder, and onion powder to create the BBQ sauce.

4. Brush a generous amount of BBQ sauce over both sides of the ribs, reserving some sauce for basting during cooking.
5. Place the ribs in a single layer on the air fryer rack, meaty side up.
6. Roast the ribs in the preheated oven for 1 hour, basting with additional BBQ sauce every 20 minutes.
7. After 1 hour, increase the temperature to 375°F and continue roasting for another 20-30 minutes, or until the ribs are tender and caramelized.
8. Once cooked, remove the ribs from the air fryer and let them rest for a few minutes before slicing and serving.

Nutritional Information (per serving):

- Calories: 600
- Protein: 35g
- Total Fats: 40g
- Fiber: 1g
- Carbohydrates: 20g

Garlic Rosemary Lamb Chops

Time to Prepare: 10 minutes
Cooking Time: 15 minutes
Number of Servings: 4

Ingredients:

- 8 lamb chops
- 4 cloves garlic, minced
- 2 tablespoons chopped fresh rosemary
- 2 tablespoons olive oil
- Salt and pepper, to taste

Instructions List:

1. Preheat your Ninja Foodi Digital Air Fryer Oven to 375°F.
2. In a small bowl, combine the minced garlic, chopped fresh rosemary, olive oil, salt, and pepper to create a marinade.
3. Rub the marinade over both sides of the lamb chops, ensuring they are evenly coated.
4. Place the lamb chops in a single layer in the air fryer basket.
5. Air fry for 12-15 minutes, flipping halfway through cooking, until the lamb chops are cooked to your desired doneness.
6. Once cooked, remove the lamb chops from the air fryer and let them rest for a few minutes before serving.

Nutritional Information (per serving):

- Calories: 350
- Protein: 25g
- Total Fats: 25g
- Fiber: 1g
- Carbohydrates: 1g

Crispy Beef Tacos

Time to Prepare: 20 minutes
Cooking Time: 10 minutes
Number of Servings: 4

Ingredients:

- 1 lb ground beef
- 1 packet taco seasoning
- 1 cup of shredded cheddar cheese
- 8 small corn tortillas
- Non-stick cooking spray
- Optional toppings: shredded lettuce, diced tomatoes, sour cream, salsa, chopped cilantro

Instructions List:

1. Preheat your Ninja Foodi Digital Air Fryer Oven to 375°F.
2. In a skillet over medium heat, cook the ground beef until browned and cooked through. Drain excess fat.
3. Add the taco seasoning to the cooked ground beef according to the packet instructions. Stir to combine.
4. Lay out the corn tortillas on a flat surface. Place a spoonful of the seasoned ground beef

in the center of each tortilla, then top with shredded cheddar cheese.

5. Fold the tortillas in half to create taco shapes.
6. Lightly spray the air fryer basket with non-stick cooking spray.
7. Arrange the filled tacos in a single layer in the air fryer basket, ensuring they are not overlapping.
8. Air fry for 8-10 minutes, or until the tacos are crispy and golden brown.
9. Remove the tacos from the air fryer and let them cool for a few minutes before serving.
10. Serve with optional toppings such as shredded lettuce, diced tomatoes, sour cream, salsa, and chopped cilantro.

Nutritional Information (per serving):

- Calories: 400
- Protein: 20g
- Total Fats: 20g
- Fiber: 3g
- Carbohydrates: 30g

Herb-Crusted Pork Tenderloin

Time to Prepare: 15 minutes
Cooking Time: 25 minutes
Number of Servings: 4

Ingredients:

- 1 lb pork tenderloin
- 2 tablespoons Dijon mustard
- 2 tablespoons chopped fresh herbs (such as rosemary, thyme, and parsley)
- 2 cloves garlic, minced
- 2 tablespoons breadcrumbs
- 1 tablespoon olive oil
- Salt and pepper, to taste

Instructions List:

1. Preheat your Ninja Foodi Digital Air Fryer Oven to 375°F on the Roast setting.
2. In a small bowl, mix together the Dijon mustard, chopped fresh herbs, minced garlic, breadcrumbs, olive oil, salt, and pepper to form a paste.
3. Pat the pork tenderloin dry with paper towels, then spread the herb paste evenly over the surface of the tenderloin.
4. Place the pork tenderloin on the air fryer rack.
5. Roast in the preheated oven for 20-25 minutes, or until the internal temperature reaches 145°F, turning halfway through cooking.
6. Once cooked, remove the pork tenderloin from the air fryer and let it rest for a few minutes before slicing.
7. Serve slices of the herb-crusted pork tenderloin with your favorite sides.

Nutritional Information (per serving):

- Calories: 250
- Protein: 30g
- Total Fats: 10g
- Fiber: 1g
- Carbohydrates: 5g

Beef Kebabs

Time to Prepare: 20 minutes
Cooking Time: 15 minutes
Number of Servings: 4

Ingredients:

- 1 lb beef sirloin or tenderloin, cut into 1-inch cubes
- 1 bell pepper, cut into 1-inch pieces
- 1 red onion, cut into 1-inch pieces
- 8 cherry tomatoes
- 8 wooden or metal skewers
- 2 tablespoons olive oil
- 2 cloves garlic, minced
- 1 teaspoon of paprika

- 1 teaspoon of cumin
- 1/2 teaspoon of chili powder
- Salt and pepper, to taste

Instructions List:

1. Preheat your Ninja Foodi Digital Air Fryer Oven to 375°F.
2. If using wooden skewers, soak them in water for at least 30 minutes to prevent burning.
3. In a small bowl, mix together the olive oil, minced garlic, paprika, cumin, chili powder, salt, and pepper to create a marinade.
4. Thread the beef cubes, bell pepper pieces, red onion pieces, and cherry tomatoes onto the skewers, alternating the ingredients.
5. Brush the marinade over the kebabs, ensuring they are evenly coated.
6. Place the kebabs on the air fryer rack, leaving a little space between each one.
7. Air fry for 12-15 minutes, turning halfway through cooking, until the beef is cooked to your desired doneness and the vegetables are tender.
8. Once cooked, remove the kebabs from the air fryer and let them rest for a few minutes before serving.
9. Serve the beef kebabs with rice, salad, or your favorite side dishes.

Nutritional Information (per serving):

- Calories: 300
- Protein: 25g
- Total Fats: 15g
- Fiber: 3g
- Carbohydrates: 10g

Sweet and Sour Pork Bites

Time to Prepare: 20 minutes
Cooking Time: 15 minutes
Number of Servings: 4

Ingredients:

- 1 lb pork tenderloin, cut into bite-sized pieces
- 1 bell pepper, diced
- 1 onion, diced
- 1 cup of pineapple chunks
- 1/2 cup of sweet and sour sauce
- 2 tablespoons soy sauce
- 1 tablespoon cornstarch
- 1 tablespoon water
- Salt and pepper, to taste

Instructions List:

1. Preheat your Ninja Foodi Digital Air Fryer Oven to 375°F.
2. In a small bowl, mix together the sweet and sour sauce, soy sauce, cornstarch, and water to create the sauce.
3. Season the pork pieces with salt and pepper.
4. Place the pork, bell pepper, onion, and pineapple chunks in a large bowl. Pour the sauce over the mixture and toss until everything is evenly coated.
5. Arrange the coated pork, bell pepper, onion, and pineapple in a single layer in the air fryer basket.
6. Air fry for 12-15 minutes, shaking the basket halfway through cooking, until the pork is cooked through and the vegetables are tender.
7. Once cooked, remove the sweet and sour pork bites from the air fryer and serve immediately.

Nutritional Information (per serving):

- Calories: 350
- Protein: 25g
- Total Fats: 10g
- Fiber: 2g
- Carbohydrates: 30g

Pork Schnitzel

Time to Prepare: 15 minutes
Cooking Time: 12 minutes
Number of Servings: 4

Ingredients:

- 4 pork loin chops, boneless and thinly sliced
- 1 cup of breadcrumbs
- 2 eggs, beaten
- 1/4 cup of all-purpose flour
- 1 teaspoon of paprika
- 1/2 teaspoon of garlic powder
- Salt and pepper, to taste
- Cooking spray

Instructions List:

1. Preheat your Ninja Foodi Digital Air Fryer Oven to 400°F.
2. Place the breadcrumbs in a shallow dish. In another shallow dish, beat the eggs. In a third shallow dish, combine the flour, paprika, garlic powder, salt, and pepper.
3. Dredge each pork chop in the flour mixture, then dip it into the beaten eggs, and finally coat it with the breadcrumbs, pressing gently to adhere.
4. Spray the air fryer basket with cooking spray. Place the breaded pork chops in a single layer in the basket, ensuring they are not touching.
5. Air fry for 6 minutes, then flip the pork chops and air fry for an additional 6 minutes, or until golden brown and cooked through.
6. Once cooked, remove the pork schnitzel from the air fryer and serve hot.

Nutritional Information (per serving):

- Calories: 350
- Protein: 30g
- Total Fats: 15g
- Fiber: 2g
- Carbohydrates: 20g

Beef and Mushroom Stuffed Peppers

Time to Prepare: 20 minutes
Cooking Time: 25 minutes
Number of Servings: 4

Ingredients:

- 4 large bell peppers, any color
- 1 lb ground beef
- 1 onion, diced
- 2 cloves garlic, minced
- 8 oz mushrooms, finely chopped
- 1 cup of cooked rice
- 1 cup of shredded cheese (such as cheddar or mozzarella)
- 1 tablespoon olive oil
- 1 teaspoon of paprika
- Salt and pepper, to taste
- Fresh parsley, chopped (for garnish, optional)

Instructions List:

1. Preheat your Ninja Foodi Digital Air Fryer Oven to 375°F on the Bake setting.
2. Cut the tops off the bell peppers and remove the seeds and membranes. Place the hollowed-out peppers in a baking dish.
3. In a skillet over medium heat, heat the olive oil. Add the diced onion and minced garlic, and cook until softened.
4. Add the ground beef to the skillet and cook until browned, breaking it apart with a spoon as it cooks.
5. Add the chopped mushrooms to the skillet and cook until they release their moisture and start to brown.
6. Stir in the cooked rice and paprika. Season with salt and pepper to taste.
7. Spoon the beef and mushroom mixture into the hollowed-out peppers, pressing down gently to pack the filling.

8. Sprinkle shredded cheese over the top of each stuffed pepper.
9. Place the baking dish with the stuffed peppers in the preheated air fryer oven.
10. Bake for 20-25 minutes, or until the peppers are tender and the cheese is melted and bubbly.
11. Once cooked, remove the stuffed peppers from the air fryer oven and garnish with chopped parsley if desired before serving.

Nutritional Information (per serving):

- Calories: 400
- Protein: 25g
- Total Fats: 20g
- Fiber: 5g
- Carbohydrates: 25g

Korean BBQ Beef Strips

Time to Prepare: 15 minutes
Cooking Time: 10 minutes
Number of Servings: 4

Ingredients:

- 1 lb beef sirloin or flank steak, thinly sliced
- 1/4 cup of soy sauce
- 2 tablespoons brown sugar
- 2 tablespoons rice vinegar
- 2 cloves garlic, minced
- 1 tablespoon sesame oil
- 1 tablespoon grated ginger
- 1 green onion, thinly sliced
- 1 tablespoon sesame seeds (optional, for garnish)

Instructions List:

1. In a bowl, whisk together the soy sauce, brown sugar, rice vinegar, minced garlic, sesame oil, and grated ginger to make the marinade.
2. Place the thinly sliced beef strips in a shallow dish or resealable plastic bag. Pour the marinade over the beef, ensuring it is evenly coated. Marinate for at least 30 minutes, or overnight in the refrigerator for maximum flavor.
3. Preheat your Ninja Foodi Digital Air Fryer Oven on the Broil setting.
4. Remove the marinated beef from the refrigerator and let it come to room temperature while the oven preheats.
5. Once the oven is preheated, arrange the marinated beef strips on the air fryer rack in a single layer, ensuring they are not overlapping.
6. Broil for 8-10 minutes, flipping the beef strips halfway through cooking, until they are caramelized and cooked to your desired level of doneness.
7. Once cooked, remove the Korean BBQ beef strips from the air fryer oven and sprinkle with thinly sliced green onions and sesame seeds if desired.

Nutritional Information (per serving):

- Calories: 300
- Protein: 25g
- Total Fats: 15g
- Fiber: 1g
- Carbohydrates: 10g

Bacon-Wrapped Filet Mignon

Time to Prepare: 10 minutes
Cooking Time: 15 minutes
Number of Servings: 2

Ingredients:

- 2 filet mignon steaks, about 6 oz each
- 4 slices bacon
- Salt and pepper, to taste
- Cooking spray

Instructions List:

1. Preheat your Ninja Foodi Digital Air Fryer Oven to 400°F on the Air Fry setting.

2. Season the filet mignon steaks with salt and pepper to taste.
3. Wrap each filet mignon steak with 2 slices of bacon, ensuring the bacon is wrapped securely around the steak.
4. Lightly coat the air fryer basket with cooking spray. Place the bacon-wrapped filet mignon steaks in the basket, leaving some space between each steak.
5. Air fry for 12-15 minutes, flipping the steaks halfway through cooking, until the bacon is crispy and the filet mignon reaches your desired level of doneness.
6. Once cooked, remove the bacon-wrapped filet mignon from the air fryer oven and let them rest for a few minutes before serving.

Nutritional Information (per serving):

- Calories: 450
- Protein: 30g
- Total Fats: 35g
- Fiber: 0g
- Carbohydrates: 0g

Pulled Pork Sliders

Time to Prepare: 15 minutes
Cooking Time: 4 hours (for slow-cooking the pork)
Number of Servings: 6

Ingredients:

- 2 lbs pork shoulder or pork butt
- 1 cup of barbecue sauce
- 1/2 cup of chicken broth or water
- 1 tablespoon brown sugar
- 1 teaspoon of garlic powder
- 1 teaspoon of onion powder
- Salt and pepper, to taste
- 12 slider buns
- Coleslaw, for topping (optional)

Instructions List:

1. Season the pork shoulder or pork butt with salt, pepper, garlic powder, and onion powder.
2. Place the seasoned pork in the Ninja Foodi Digital Air Fryer Oven's cooking pot. Add the chicken broth or water.
3. Close the pressure lid and set the valve to SEAL. Select the Slow Cook function and set the time for 4 hours.
4. Once the pork is cooked, carefully release the pressure and remove the lid.
5. Using two forks, shred the cooked pork in the cooking pot. Remove any excess liquid.
6. Stir in the barbecue sauce and brown sugar until the pork is evenly coated.
7. Preheat the Ninja Foodi Digital Air Fryer Oven to 375°F on the Bake setting.
8. Split the slider buns and place them on a baking tray lined with parchment paper.
9. Spoon the pulled pork mixture onto the bottom half of each slider bun.
10. Place the top half of the slider buns on top of the pulled pork.
11. Bake for 5-7 minutes, or until the sliders are heated through and the buns are slightly toasted.
12. Serve the pulled pork sliders hot, optionally topped with coleslaw.

Nutritional Information (per serving):

- Calories: 450
- Protein: 25g
- Total Fats: 20g
- Fiber: 2g
- Carbohydrates: 40g

Beef Wellington Bites

Time to Prepare: 30 minutes
Cooking Time: 20 minutes
Number of Servings: 4

Ingredients:

- 1 sheet puff pastry, thawed

- 4 beef tenderloin medallions, about 4 oz each
- Salt and pepper, to taste
- 2 tablespoons Dijon mustard
- 4 slices prosciutto
- 1 tablespoon olive oil
- 1 egg, beaten (for egg wash)

Instructions List:

1. Preheat your Ninja Foodi Digital Air Fryer Oven to 375°F on the Air Fry setting.
2. Season the beef tenderloin medallions with salt and pepper.
3. Heat the olive oil in a skillet over medium-high heat. Sear the beef tenderloin medallions for 1-2 minutes on each side until browned. Remove from heat and let them cool slightly.
4. Roll out the puff pastry sheet on a lightly floured surface. Cut it into 4 equal squares.
5. Spread a thin layer of Dijon mustard on each square of puff pastry.
6. Place a slice of prosciutto on top of the Dijon mustard.
7. Put a seared beef tenderloin medallion on top of the prosciutto.
8. Fold the edges of the puff pastry square over the beef tenderloin to enclose it completely.
9. Brush the edges of the puff pastry with the beaten egg to seal.
10. Place the beef wellington bites in the air fryer basket, seam side down.
11. Air fry for 15-20 minutes, or until the puff pastry is golden brown and crispy.
12. Once cooked, remove the beef wellington bites from the air fryer oven and let them cool for a few minutes before serving.

Nutritional Information (per serving):

- Calories: 450
- Protein: 25g
- Total Fats: 30g
- Fiber: 1g
- Carbohydrates: 25g

Teriyaki Glazed Pork Chops

Time to Prepare: 10 minutes
Cooking Time: 20 minutes
Number of Servings: 4

Ingredients:

- 4 bone-in pork chops, about 6 oz each
- Salt and pepper, to taste
- 1/2 cup of teriyaki sauce
- 2 tablespoons honey
- 1 tablespoon sesame oil
- 2 cloves garlic, minced
- 1 teaspoon of ginger, grated
- Sesame seeds, for garnish (optional)
- Sliced green onions, for garnish (optional)

Instructions List:

1. Preheat your Ninja Foodi Digital Air Fryer Oven to 400°F on the Broil setting.
2. Season the pork chops with salt and pepper on both sides.
3. In a small bowl, mix together the teriyaki sauce, honey, sesame oil, minced garlic, and grated ginger to make the glaze.
4. Place the pork chops on the air fryer basket or tray.
5. Brush the pork chops with the teriyaki glaze, making sure to coat them evenly.
6. Place the pork chops in the preheated air fryer oven and broil for 10 minutes.
7. After 10 minutes, flip the pork chops over and brush them with more teriyaki glaze.
8. Broil for another 10 minutes, or until the pork chops are cooked through and caramelized on the outside.
9. Once cooked, remove the pork chops from the air fryer oven and let them rest for a few minutes before serving.

10. Garnish with sesame seeds and sliced green onions, if desired.

Nutritional Information (per serving):

- Calories: 350
- Protein: 30g
- Total Fats: 15g
- Fiber: 0g
- Carbohydrates: 20g

Chapter 4: Fish & Seafood

Lemon Garlic Shrimp Skewers

Time to Prepare: 15 minutes
Cooking Time: 10 minutes
Number of Servings: 4

Ingredients:

- 1 lb large shrimp, peeled and deveined
- 2 tablespoons olive oil
- 2 cloves garlic, minced
- Zest of 1 lemon
- Juice of 1 lemon
- 1 teaspoon of dried oregano
- Salt and pepper, to taste
- Wooden skewers, soaked in water for 30 minutes

Instructions List:

1. Preheat your Ninja Foodi Digital Air Fryer Oven to 400°F on the Air Fry setting.
2. In a bowl, combine the olive oil, minced garlic, lemon zest, lemon juice, dried oregano, salt, and pepper.
3. Add the peeled and deveined shrimp to the bowl and toss to coat them evenly with the marinade.
4. Thread the marinated shrimp onto the soaked wooden skewers, dividing them evenly.
5. Place the shrimp skewers in the air fryer basket or tray, making sure they are not overcrowded.
6. Air fry the shrimp skewers at 400°F for 5 minutes.
7. After 5 minutes, flip the skewers over and air fry for an additional 5 minutes, or until the shrimp are pink and cooked through.
8. Once cooked, remove the shrimp skewers from the air fryer oven and serve immediately.

Nutritional Information (per serving):

- Calories: 180
- Protein: 25g
- Total Fats: 7g
- Fiber: 1g
- Carbohydrates: 3g

Fish Tacos

Time to Prepare: 20 minutes
Cooking Time: 12 minutes
Number of Servings: 4

Ingredients:

- 1 lb white fish fillets (such as cod or tilapia)
- 1/2 cup of all-purpose flour
- 1 teaspoon of chili powder
- 1 teaspoon of garlic powder
- 1/2 teaspoon of paprika
- Salt and pepper, to taste
- 2 eggs, beaten
- 1 cup of breadcrumbs
- Cooking spray
- 8 small flour tortillas
- Shredded cabbage
- Sliced avocado
- Salsa
- Lime wedges

Instructions List:

1. Preheat your Ninja Foodi Digital Air Fryer Oven to 400°F on the Air Fry setting.
2. Cut the fish fillets into strips or bite-sized pieces.
3. In a shallow dish, mix together the all-purpose flour, chili powder, garlic powder, paprika, salt, and pepper.
4. In another shallow dish, place the beaten eggs.

5. Place the breadcrumbs in a third shallow dish.
6. Dredge the fish pieces in the seasoned flour mixture, then dip them into the beaten eggs, and finally coat them in the breadcrumbs, pressing gently to adhere.
7. Place the breaded fish pieces on the air fryer basket or tray in a single layer.
8. Lightly spray the breaded fish with cooking spray.
9. Air fry the fish at 400°F for 6 minutes.
10. After 6 minutes, flip the fish pieces over and air fry for another 6 minutes, or until they are golden brown and crispy.
11. Warm the flour tortillas in the air fryer for 1-2 minutes before assembling the tacos.
12. To assemble the tacos, place some shredded cabbage on each tortilla, top with the air-fried fish pieces, sliced avocado, and salsa.
13. Serve the fish tacos with lime wedges on the side for squeezing.

Nutritional Information (per serving):

- Calories: 420
- Protein: 24g
- Total Fats: 16g
- Fiber: 5g
- Carbohydrates: 44g

Crispy Coconut Shrimp

Time to Prepare: 15 minutes
Cooking Time: 10 minutes
Number of Servings: 4

Ingredients:

- 1 lb large shrimp, peeled and deveined
- 1/2 cup of all-purpose flour
- 2 eggs, beaten
- 1 cup of shredded coconut
- 1 cup of panko breadcrumbs
- 1/2 teaspoon of garlic powder
- 1/2 teaspoon of paprika
- Salt and pepper, to taste
- Cooking spray

Instructions List:

1. Preheat your Ninja Foodi Digital Air Fryer Oven to 400°F on the Air Fry setting.
2. In a shallow dish, combine the shredded coconut, panko breadcrumbs, garlic powder, paprika, salt, and pepper.
3. Place the all-purpose flour in another shallow dish and the beaten eggs in a third shallow dish.
4. Dredge each shrimp in the flour, shaking off any excess.
5. Dip the floured shrimp into the beaten eggs, allowing any excess to drip off.
6. Coat the shrimp in the coconut breadcrumb mixture, pressing gently to adhere.
7. Place the breaded shrimp on the air fryer basket or tray in a single layer.
8. Lightly spray the breaded shrimp with cooking spray.
9. Air fry the shrimp at 400°F for 5 minutes.
10. After 5 minutes, flip the shrimp over and air fry for an additional 5 minutes, or until they are golden brown and crispy.
11. Once cooked, remove the shrimp from the air fryer oven and serve immediately.

Nutritional Information (per serving):

- Calories: 380
- Protein: 20g
- Total Fats: 18g
- Fiber: 3g
- Carbohydrates: 32g

Herb-Crusted Salmon Fillets

Time to Prepare: 10 minutes
Cooking Time: 12 minutes
Number of Servings: 4

Ingredients:

- 4 salmon fillets
- 1/4 cup of breadcrumbs
- 2 tablespoons grated Parmesan cheese
- 1 tablespoon chopped fresh parsley
- 1 tablespoon chopped fresh dill
- 1 tablespoon chopped fresh chives
- 1 tablespoon olive oil
- 1 teaspoon of lemon zest
- Salt and pepper, to taste
- Lemon wedges, for serving

Instructions List:

1. Preheat your Ninja Foodi Digital Air Fryer Oven to 400°F on the Roast setting.
2. In a small bowl, combine the breadcrumbs, Parmesan cheese, chopped parsley, dill, chives, olive oil, lemon zest, salt, and pepper to make the herb crust mixture.
3. Pat the salmon fillets dry with paper towels.
4. Press the herb crust mixture onto the top of each salmon fillet, covering the entire surface evenly.
5. Place the herb-crusted salmon fillets on the air fryer basket or tray.
6. Roast the salmon at 400°F for 12 minutes, or until the fish is cooked through and flakes easily with a fork.
7. Once cooked, remove the salmon fillets from the air fryer oven and let them rest for a few minutes before serving.
8. Serve the herb-crusted salmon fillets with lemon wedges on the side.

Nutritional Information (per serving):

- Calories: 290
- Protein: 24g
- Total Fats: 16g
- Fiber: 1g
- Carbohydrates: 7g

Calamari

Time to Prepare: 15 minutes
Cooking Time: 10 minutes
Number of Servings: 4

Ingredients:

- 1 lb calamari rings, thawed if frozen
- 1/2 cup of all-purpose flour
- 2 eggs, beaten
- 1 cup of breadcrumbs
- 1 teaspoon of paprika
- 1/2 teaspoon of garlic powder
- 1/2 teaspoon of dried oregano
- Salt and pepper, to taste
- Cooking spray
- Marinara sauce, for serving

Instructions List:

1. Preheat your Ninja Foodi Digital Air Fryer Oven to 400°F on the Air Fry setting.
2. In a shallow dish, combine the breadcrumbs, paprika, garlic powder, dried oregano, salt, and pepper.
3. Place the all-purpose flour in another shallow dish and the beaten eggs in a third shallow dish.
4. Dredge the calamari rings in the flour, shaking off any excess.
5. Dip the floured calamari rings into the beaten eggs, allowing any excess to drip off.
6. Coat the calamari rings in the seasoned breadcrumb mixture, pressing gently to adhere.
7. Place the breaded calamari rings on the air fryer basket or tray in a single layer.
8. Lightly spray the breaded calamari rings with cooking spray.
9. Air fry the calamari at 400°F for 5 minutes.
10. After 5 minutes, shake the basket or flip the calamari rings over and air fry for an

additional 5 minutes, or until they are golden brown and crispy.

11. Once cooked, remove the calamari from the air fryer oven and serve immediately with marinara sauce for dipping.

Nutritional Information (per serving):

- Calories: 280
- Protein: 22g
- Total Fats: 8g
- Fiber: 2g
- Carbohydrates: 29g

Garlic Butter Scallops

Time to Prepare: 10 minutes
Cooking Time: 8 minutes
Number of Servings: 4

Ingredients:

- 1 lb fresh scallops, patted dry
- 4 tablespoons unsalted butter, melted
- 4 cloves garlic, minced
- 1 tablespoon fresh lemon juice
- Salt and pepper, to taste
- Fresh parsley, chopped (for garnish)
- Lemon wedges, for serving

Instructions List:

1. Preheat your Ninja Foodi Digital Air Fryer Oven to 400°F on the Broil setting.
2. In a small bowl, combine the melted butter, minced garlic, and fresh lemon juice.
3. Season the scallops with salt and pepper on both sides.
4. Place the scallops on the air fryer tray or basket in a single layer.
5. Spoon the garlic butter mixture evenly over the scallops.
6. Place the tray or basket in the air fryer oven and broil for 4 minutes.
7. After 4 minutes, carefully flip the scallops over using tongs and broil for an additional 4 minutes, or until they are opaque and lightly browned.
8. Once cooked, remove the scallops from the air fryer oven and transfer them to a serving platter.
9. Garnish with chopped parsley and serve with lemon wedges on the side.

Nutritional Information (per serving):

- Calories: 215
- Protein: 19g
- Total Fats: 12g
- Fiber: 0g
- Carbohydrates: 5g

Teriyaki Glazed Salmon

Time to Prepare: 15 minutes
Cooking Time: 15 minutes
Number of Servings: 4

Ingredients:

- 4 salmon fillets
- ½ cup teriyaki sauce
- 2 tablespoons honey
- 2 cloves garlic, minced
- 1 teaspoon of grated ginger
- 2 green onions, thinly sliced
- Sesame seeds, for garnish

Instructions List:

1. Preheat your Ninja Foodi Digital Air Fryer Oven to 375°F on the Bake setting.
2. In a small bowl, whisk together teriyaki sauce, honey, minced garlic, and grated ginger to make the teriyaki glaze.
3. Place the salmon fillets on a baking tray lined with parchment paper.
4. Brush the teriyaki glaze generously over the salmon fillets.

5. Place the tray in the air fryer oven and bake for 12-15 minutes, or until the salmon is cooked through and flakes easily with a fork.
6. Once cooked, remove the salmon from the air fryer oven and sprinkle with sliced green onions and sesame seeds.
7. Serve the teriyaki glazed salmon hot, accompanied by your favorite side dishes.

Nutritional Information (per serving):

- Calories: 297
- Protein: 24g
- Total Fats: 14g
- Fiber: 0.5g
- Carbohydrates: 18g

Crab Cakes

Time to Prepare: 20 minutes
Cooking Time: 15 minutes
Number of Servings: 4

Ingredients:

- 1 pound lump crabmeat, drained
- 1 egg, beaten
- 1/4 cup of mayonnaise
- 1 tablespoon Dijon mustard
- 1 tablespoon Worcestershire sauce
- 1 teaspoon of Old Bay seasoning
- 1/2 cup of breadcrumbs
- 2 green onions, finely chopped
- 1/4 cup of chopped fresh parsley
- Salt and pepper to taste
- Olive oil spray

Instructions List:

1. In a large mixing bowl, combine the lump crabmeat, beaten egg, mayonnaise, Dijon mustard, Worcestershire sauce, Old Bay seasoning, breadcrumbs, chopped green onions, chopped parsley, salt, and pepper. Mix until well fat.
2. Shape the crab mixture into 8 evenly sized patties.
3. Preheat your Ninja Foodi Digital Air Fryer Oven to 375°F on the Air Fry setting.
4. Lightly coat both sides of the crab cakes with olive oil spray.
5. Place the crab cakes in the air fryer basket in a single layer, making sure they are not touching each other.
6. Air fry the crab cakes for 12-15 minutes, flipping halfway through the cooking time, until they are golden brown and crispy on the outside and heated through.
7. Once cooked, remove the crab cakes from the air fryer basket and serve hot, garnished with lemon wedges and your favorite dipping sauce.

Nutritional Information (per serving):

- Calories: 241
- Protein: 18g
- Total Fats: 14g
- Fiber: 1g
- Carbohydrates: 11g

Shrimp and Vegetable Stir-Fry

Time to Prepare: 20 minutes
Cooking Time: 15 minutes
Number of Servings: 4

Ingredients:

- 1 lb large shrimp, peeled and deveined
- 2 cups of mixed vegetables (such as bell peppers, broccoli, snap peas, and carrots), sliced
- 2 cloves garlic, minced
- 1 tablespoon ginger, minced
- 2 tablespoons soy sauce
- 1 tablespoon hoisin sauce
- 1 tablespoon oyster sauce
- 1 tablespoon sesame oil

- 1 tablespoon olive oil
- Salt and pepper to taste
- Cooked rice or noodles, for serving
- Sesame seeds and chopped green onions, for garnish

Instructions List:

1. Preheat your Ninja Foodi Digital Air Fryer Oven to 400°F on the Broil setting.
2. In a small bowl, whisk together the soy sauce, hoisin sauce, and oyster sauce. Set aside.
3. Heat olive oil in a skillet over medium-high heat. Add minced garlic and ginger, and sauté for 1-2 minutes until fragrant.
4. Add the mixed vegetables to the skillet and stir-fry for 3-4 minutes until they begin to soften.
5. Push the vegetables to one side of the skillet and add the shrimp to the other side. Cook the shrimp for 2-3 minutes on each side until pink and cooked through.
6. Pour the sauce over the shrimp and vegetables in the skillet. Stir to combine and cook for an additional 1-2 minutes until heated through.
7. Remove the skillet from heat and drizzle with sesame oil. Toss to coat evenly.
8. Transfer the shrimp and vegetable stir-fry to a serving dish.
9. Garnish with sesame seeds and chopped green onions.
10. Serve hot over cooked rice or noodles.

Nutritional Information (per serving):

- Calories: 245
- Protein: 25g
- Total Fats: 9g
- Fiber: 4g
- Carbohydrates: 16g

Lobster Tails

Time to Prepare: 10 minutes
Cooking Time: 10 minutes
Number of Servings: 2

Ingredients:

- 2 lobster tails, thawed if frozen
- 2 tablespoons butter, melted
- 1 teaspoon of garlic powder
- 1 teaspoon of paprika
- Salt and pepper to taste
- Lemon wedges, for serving
- Chopped parsley, for garnish

Instructions List:

1. Preheat your Ninja Foodi Digital Air Fryer Oven to 400°F on the Air Fry setting.
2. Use kitchen shears to cut along the top of each lobster tail shell.
3. Carefully lift the lobster meat from the shell, keeping it attached at the base.
4. Place the lobster tails on a cutting board, and use a knife to make a shallow slit down the center of the meat to butterfly it.
5. In a small bowl, mix together the melted butter, garlic powder, paprika, salt, and pepper.
6. Brush the seasoned butter mixture over the exposed lobster meat.
7. Place the lobster tails in the air fryer basket or on the air fryer tray, shell side down.
8. Air fry the lobster tails at 400°F for 8-10 minutes, or until the meat is opaque and cooked through.
9. Carefully remove the lobster tails from the air fryer.
10. Serve hot with lemon wedges and garnish with chopped parsley.

Nutritional Information (per serving):

- Calories: 225
- Protein: 24g

- Total Fats: 14g
- Fiber: 0g
- Carbohydrates: 1g

Blackened Tilapia

Time to Prepare: 10 minutes
Cooking Time: 10 minutes
Number of Servings: 4

Ingredients:

- 4 tilapia fillets
- 2 tablespoons olive oil
- 2 teaspoons of paprika
- 1 teaspoon of garlic powder
- 1 teaspoon of onion powder
- 1 teaspoon of thyme
- 1 teaspoon of oregano
- 1/2 teaspoon of cayenne pepper
- Salt and pepper to taste
- Lemon wedges, for serving
- Chopped parsley, for garnish

Instructions List:

1. Preheat your Ninja Foodi Digital Air Fryer Oven to 400°F on the Broil setting.
2. In a small bowl, mix together the olive oil, paprika, garlic powder, onion powder, thyme, oregano, cayenne pepper, salt, and pepper to form a paste.
3. Rub the spice paste evenly over both sides of each tilapia fillet.
4. Place the seasoned tilapia fillets on the air fryer tray or in the air fryer basket.
5. Place the tray or basket in the lowest position in the air fryer.
6. Broil the tilapia for 8-10 minutes, or until the fish is cooked through and the spices are blackened.
7. Carefully remove the tilapia from the air fryer.
8. Serve hot with lemon wedges and garnish with chopped parsley.

Nutritional Information (per serving):

- Calories: 170
- Protein: 25g
- Total Fats: 7g
- Fiber: 1g
- Carbohydrates: 2g

Stuffed Clams

Time to Prepare: 20 minutes
Cooking Time: 10 minutes
Number of Servings: 4

Ingredients:

- 16 large clams, scrubbed clean
- 1/4 cup of breadcrumbs
- 2 tablespoons grated Parmesan cheese
- 2 cloves garlic, minced
- 2 tablespoons chopped fresh parsley
- 1 tablespoon olive oil
- Salt and pepper to taste
- Lemon wedges, for serving

Instructions List:

1. Preheat your Ninja Foodi Digital Air Fryer Oven to 375°F on the Air Fry setting.
2. In a bowl, combine the breadcrumbs, Parmesan cheese, minced garlic, chopped parsley, olive oil, salt, and pepper.
3. Gently pry open each clamshell and remove the clam meat. Set aside the clam meat and clean the shells.
4. Chop the clam meat and mix it into the breadcrumb mixture.
5. Stuff each clam shell with the breadcrumb mixture, pressing it down gently.
6. Arrange the stuffed clams in the air fryer basket or on the air fryer tray.

7. Air fry the stuffed clams at 375°F for 8-10 minutes, or until the breadcrumbs are golden brown and crispy.
8. Carefully remove the stuffed clams from the air fryer.
9. Serve hot with lemon wedges.

Nutritional Information (per serving):

- Calories: 180
- Protein: 15g
- Total Fats: 6g
- Fiber: 2g
- Carbohydrates: 15g

Fish and Chips

Time to Prepare: 15 minutes
Cooking Time: 20 minutes
Number of Servings: 4

Ingredients:

- 4 fillets of white fish (such as cod or haddock), about 6 ounces each
- 1 cup of all-purpose flour
- 1 teaspoon of baking powder
- 1/2 teaspoon of salt
- 1/2 teaspoon of black pepper
- 1/2 cup of cold water
- 1 large egg
- 1 cup of breadcrumbs
- Cooking spray
- Lemon wedges, for serving
- Tartar sauce, for serving
- French fries, for serving

Instructions List:

1. Preheat your Ninja Foodi Digital Air Fryer Oven to 400°F on the Air Fry setting.
2. Pat the fish fillets dry with paper towels and season them with salt and pepper.
3. In a shallow dish, mix together the flour, baking powder, salt, and black pepper.
4. In another shallow dish, whisk together the cold water and egg.
5. Place the breadcrumbs in a third shallow dish.
6. Dredge each fish fillet in the flour mixture, shaking off any excess.
7. Dip the floured fish fillets into the egg mixture, allowing any excess to drip off.
8. Coat the fish fillets evenly with breadcrumbs, pressing gently to adhere.
9. Lightly coat the air fryer basket or tray with cooking spray.
10. Arrange the breaded fish fillets in a single layer in the air fryer basket or on the air fryer tray.
11. Air fry the fish at 400°F for 12-15 minutes, flipping halfway through, until golden brown and crispy.
12. While the fish is cooking, prepare the French fries according to package instructions.
13. Serve the air-fried fish and chips hot with lemon wedges and tartar sauce on the side.

Nutritional Information (per serving):

- Calories: 470
- Protein: 32g
- Total Fats: 12g
- Fiber: 3g
- Carbohydrates: 56g

Spicy Tuna Patties

Time to Prepare: 15 minutes
Cooking Time: 15 minutes
Number of Servings: 4

Ingredients:

- 2 cans (5 ounces each) tuna, drained
- 1/4 cup of breadcrumbs
- 1/4 cup of finely chopped onion

- 1/4 cup of finely chopped bell pepper
- 1 large egg, beaten
- 2 tablespoons mayonnaise
- 1 tablespoon Dijon mustard
- 1 tablespoon Sriracha sauce
- 1 teaspoon of lemon juice
- 1/2 teaspoon of garlic powder
- 1/2 teaspoon of paprika
- Salt and pepper, to taste
- Cooking spray

Instructions List:

1. In a mixing bowl, combine the drained tuna, breadcrumbs, chopped onion, chopped bell pepper, beaten egg, mayonnaise, Dijon mustard, Sriracha sauce, lemon juice, garlic powder, paprika, salt, and pepper. Mix until well fat.
2. Divide the tuna mixture into 4 equal portions and shape each portion into a patty.
3. Preheat your Ninja Foodi Digital Air Fryer Oven to 375°F on the Air Fry setting.
4. Lightly coat the air fryer basket or tray with cooking spray.
5. Place the tuna patties in a single layer in the air fryer basket or on the air fryer tray.
6. Air fry the tuna patties at 375°F for 12-15 minutes, flipping halfway through, until golden brown and cooked through.
7. Serve the spicy tuna patties hot with your favorite dipping sauce or on a bun as a burger.

Nutritional Information (per serving):

- Calories: 180
- Protein: 20g
- Total Fats: 7g
- Fiber: 1g
- Carbohydrates: 8g

Chapter 5: Appetizers & Snacks

Mozzarella Sticks

Time to Prepare: 15 minutes
Cooking Time: 10 minutes
Number of Servings: 4

Ingredients:

- 12 mozzarella string cheese sticks
- 1/2 cup of all-purpose flour
- 2 large eggs, beaten
- 1 cup of Italian seasoned breadcrumbs
- Cooking spray
- Marinara sauce, for dipping (optional)

Instructions List:

1. Cut the mozzarella string cheese sticks in half widthwise to create 24 shorter sticks.
2. Set up a breading station with three shallow bowls: one with all-purpose flour, one with beaten eggs, and one with Italian seasoned breadcrumbs.
3. Dredge each mozzarella stick in the flour, shaking off any excess.
4. Dip the floured mozzarella stick into the beaten eggs, allowing any excess to drip off.
5. Roll the mozzarella stick in the breadcrumbs, pressing gently to adhere the breadcrumbs to the cheese.
6. Place the breaded mozzarella sticks on a baking sheet lined with parchment paper.
7. Preheat your Ninja Foodi Digital Air Fryer Oven to 375°F on the Air Fry setting.
8. Lightly coat the air fryer basket or tray with cooking spray.
9. Arrange the breaded mozzarella sticks in a single layer in the air fryer basket or on the air fryer tray.
10. Air fry the mozzarella sticks at 375°F for 8-10 minutes, or until golden brown and crispy.
11. Serve the air-fried mozzarella sticks hot with marinara sauce for dipping, if desired.

Nutritional Information (per serving):

- Calories: 290
- Protein: 18g
- Total Fats: 15g
- Fiber: 1g
- Carbohydrates: 20g

Spicy Jalapeño Poppers

Time to Prepare: 20 minutes
Cooking Time: 10 minutes
Number of Servings: 4

Ingredients:

- 12 fresh jalapeño peppers
- 8 oz cream cheese, softened
- 1 cup of shredded cheddar cheese
- 1/2 teaspoon of garlic powder
- 1/2 teaspoon of onion powder
- 1/2 teaspoon of paprika
- Salt and pepper, to taste
- 1 cup of breadcrumbs
- Cooking spray

Instructions List:

1. Preheat your Ninja Foodi Digital Air Fryer Oven to 375°F on the Air Fry setting.
2. Cut the jalapeño peppers in half lengthwise and remove the seeds and membranes.
3. In a mixing bowl, combine the softened cream cheese, shredded cheddar cheese, garlic powder, onion powder, paprika, salt, and pepper. Mix until well fat.
4. Fill each jalapeño half with the cheese mixture, pressing gently to fill the cavity.
5. Place the breadcrumbs in a shallow bowl.
6. Dip each stuffed jalapeño half into the breadcrumbs, coating evenly.

7. Lightly coat the air fryer basket or tray with cooking spray.
8. Arrange the breaded jalapeño poppers in a single layer in the air fryer basket or on the air fryer tray.
9. Air fry the jalapeño poppers at 375°F for 8-10 minutes, or until the coating is golden brown and the peppers are tender.
10. Serve the spicy jalapeño poppers hot as a delicious appetizer or snack.

Nutritional Information (per serving):

- Calories: 280
- Protein: 9g
- Total Fats: 18g
- Fiber: 2g
- Carbohydrates: 22g

Garlic Parmesan Zucchini Fries

Time to Prepare: 15 minutes
Cooking Time: 12 minutes
Number of Servings: 4

Ingredients:

- 2 large zucchinis
- 1/2 cup of grated Parmesan cheese
- 1/2 cup of breadcrumbs
- 2 cloves garlic, minced
- 1/2 teaspoon of dried oregano
- 1/2 teaspoon of dried basil
- 1/4 teaspoon of salt
- 1/4 teaspoon of black pepper
- 2 eggs
- Cooking spray

Instructions List:

1. Preheat your Ninja Foodi Digital Air Fryer Oven to 400°F on the Air Fry setting.
2. Trim the ends of the zucchinis and cut them into thin fry-shaped pieces.
3. In a shallow bowl, combine the grated Parmesan cheese, breadcrumbs, minced garlic, dried oregano, dried basil, salt, and black pepper.
4. In another shallow bowl, beat the eggs.
5. Dip each zucchini fry into the beaten eggs, allowing any excess to drip off.
6. Coat the zucchini fry in the Parmesan breadcrumb mixture, pressing gently to adhere.
7. Lightly coat the air fryer basket or tray with cooking spray.
8. Arrange the coated zucchini fries in a single layer in the air fryer basket or on the air fryer tray.
9. Lightly spray the tops of the zucchini fries with cooking spray.
10. Air fry the zucchini fries at 400°F for 10-12 minutes, flipping halfway through, until golden brown and crispy.
11. Serve the garlic Parmesan zucchini fries hot as a tasty appetizer or side dish.

Nutritional Information (per serving):

- Calories: 160
- Protein: 9g
- Total Fats: 6g
- Fiber: 3g
- Carbohydrates: 18g

Buffalo Cauliflower Bites

Time to Prepare: 15 minutes
Cooking Time: 20 minutes
Number of Servings: 4

Ingredients:

- 1 head cauliflower, cut into florets
- 1/2 cup of all-purpose flour
- 1/2 cup of water
- 1 teaspoon of garlic powder
- 1/2 teaspoon of paprika

- 1/2 teaspoon of salt
- 1/4 teaspoon of black pepper
- 1/4 cup of hot sauce
- 2 tablespoons unsalted butter, melted
- Cooking spray

Instructions List:

1. Preheat your Ninja Foodi Digital Air Fryer Oven to 375°F on the Air Fry setting.
2. In a mixing bowl, whisk together the flour, water, garlic powder, paprika, salt, and black pepper to form a smooth batter.
3. Dip each cauliflower floret into the batter, shaking off any excess.
4. Lightly coat the air fryer basket or tray with cooking spray.
5. Arrange the battered cauliflower florets in a single layer in the air fryer basket or on the air fryer tray.
6. Air fry the cauliflower at 375°F for 15 minutes, shaking the basket or flipping the florets halfway through, until they are golden brown and crisp.
7. In a separate bowl, mix together the hot sauce and melted butter.
8. Remove the cauliflower from the air fryer and toss them in the buffalo sauce mixture until evenly coated.
9. Return the coated cauliflower to the air fryer basket or tray.
10. Air fry the cauliflower at 375°F for an additional 5 minutes to crisp up the buffalo coating.
11. Serve the buffalo cauliflower bites hot with your favorite dipping sauce.

Nutritional Information (per serving):

- Calories: 120
- Protein: 3g
- Total Fats: 5g
- Fiber: 3g
- Carbohydrates: 17g

Stuffed Mushrooms

Time to Prepare: 20 minutes
Cooking Time: 15 minutes
Number of Servings: 4

Ingredients:

- 16 large mushrooms, stems removed and reserved
- 1/2 cup of Italian seasoned bread crumbs
- 1/4 cup of grated Parmesan cheese
- 2 cloves garlic, minced
- 2 tablespoons olive oil
- 1 tablespoon chopped fresh parsley
- Salt and pepper to taste
- Cooking spray

Instructions List:

1. Preheat your Ninja Foodi Digital Air Fryer Oven to 375°F on the Air Fry setting.
2. Finely chop the mushroom stems.
3. In a mixing bowl, combine the chopped mushroom stems, bread crumbs, Parmesan cheese, minced garlic, olive oil, chopped parsley, salt, and pepper. Mix well to form a stuffing mixture.
4. Stuff each mushroom cap with the prepared stuffing mixture, pressing down gently to pack it in.
5. Lightly coat the air fryer basket or tray with cooking spray.
6. Arrange the stuffed mushrooms in a single layer in the air fryer basket or on the air fryer tray.
7. Air fry the stuffed mushrooms at 375°F for 15 minutes, or until the mushrooms are tender and the stuffing is golden brown.
8. Serve the air-fried stuffed mushrooms hot as an appetizer or side dish.

Nutritional Information (per serving):

- Calories: 110
- Protein: 4g

- Total Fats: 6g
- Fiber: 2g
- Carbohydrates: 10g

Mini Spinach and Feta Pies

Time to Prepare: 30 minutes
Cooking Time: 20 minutes
Number of Servings: 6

Ingredients:

- 1 tablespoon olive oil
- 1 small onion, finely chopped
- 2 garlic cloves, minced
- 6 cups of fresh spinach leaves
- Salt and pepper to taste
- 1/4 cup of crumbled feta cheese
- 1/4 cup of grated Parmesan cheese
- 2 sheets frozen puff pastry, thawed
- 1 egg, beaten (for egg wash)

Instructions List:

1. Preheat your Ninja Foodi Digital Air Fryer Oven to 375°F on the Bake setting.
2. Heat the olive oil in a skillet over medium heat. Add the chopped onion and garlic, and cook until softened.
3. Add the fresh spinach leaves to the skillet and cook until wilted. Season with salt and pepper to taste. Remove from heat and let cool slightly.
4. Once cooled, transfer the spinach mixture to a mixing bowl. Stir in the crumbled feta cheese and grated Parmesan cheese until well fat.
5. Roll out the thawed puff pastry sheets on a lightly floured surface. Cut each sheet into 6 squares.
6. Place a spoonful of the spinach and cheese mixture in the center of each pastry square. Fold the corners of the pastry over the filling to form small pies.
7. Place the mini pies on a baking sheet lined with parchment paper. Brush the tops with beaten egg for a golden finish.
8. Bake in the preheated air fryer oven for 20 minutes, or until the pastry is golden brown and crispy.
9. Serve the mini spinach and feta pies warm as a delightful appetizer or snack.

Nutritional Information (per serving):

- Calories: 280
- Protein: 6g
- Total Fats: 19g
- Fiber: 3g
- Carbohydrates: 23g

Cheesy Potato Skins

Time to Prepare: 20 minutes
Cooking Time: 25 minutes
Number of Servings: 4

Ingredients:

- 4 large russet potatoes
- 2 tablespoons olive oil
- Salt and pepper to taste
- 1 cup of shredded cheddar cheese
- 4 slices bacon, cooked and crumbled
- 2 green onions, thinly sliced
- Sour cream, for serving
- Fresh parsley, chopped (optional, for garnish)

Instructions List:

1. Preheat your Ninja Foodi Digital Air Fryer Oven to 400°F on the Air Fry setting.
2. Scrub the potatoes clean and pat them dry. Pierce each potato several times with a fork.
3. Rub the potatoes with olive oil and season generously with salt and pepper.
4. Place the potatoes directly on the air fryer rack or basket and cook for 25 minutes, or until tender.

5. Once the potatoes are cooked, remove them from the air fryer and let them cool slightly.
6. Slice each potato in half lengthwise and scoop out the flesh, leaving about 1/4 inch of potato on the skin.
7. Place the hollowed-out potato skins back into the air fryer basket or on the rack.
8. Fill each potato skin with shredded cheddar cheese and crumbled bacon.
9. Return the filled potato skins to the air fryer and cook for an additional 5 minutes, or until the cheese is melted and bubbly.
10. Once done, remove the potato skins from the air fryer and garnish with sliced green onions and chopped parsley, if desired.
11. Serve the cheesy potato skins hot with a dollop of sour cream on the side.

Nutritional Information (per serving):

- Calories: 380
- Protein: 14g
- Total Fats: 21g
- Fiber: 4g
- Carbohydrates: 35g

BBQ Chicken Wings

Time to Prepare: 10 minutes
Cooking Time: 20 minutes
Number of Servings: 4

Ingredients:

- 2 pounds chicken wings, split at joints, tips discarded
- 1/2 cup of barbecue sauce
- 1 tablespoon olive oil
- 1 teaspoon of garlic powder
- 1 teaspoon of onion powder
- Salt and pepper to taste
- Chopped fresh parsley, for garnish (optional)

Instructions List:

1. In a large bowl, toss the chicken wings with olive oil, garlic powder, onion powder, salt, and pepper until evenly coated.
2. Preheat your Ninja Foodi Digital Air Fryer Oven to 380°F on the Air Fry setting.
3. Arrange the seasoned chicken wings in a single layer in the air fryer basket or on the air fryer rack, ensuring they are not touching.
4. Air fry the chicken wings at 380°F for 10 minutes.
5. After 10 minutes, flip the chicken wings using tongs and air fry for an additional 10 minutes, or until crispy and golden brown.
6. Once the chicken wings are cooked through and crispy, transfer them to a clean bowl.
7. Pour the barbecue sauce over the cooked chicken wings and toss until they are evenly coated.
8. Return the sauced chicken wings to the air fryer basket or rack and air fry for an additional 5 minutes at 380°F to caramelize the sauce.
9. Once done, remove the BBQ chicken wings from the air fryer and garnish with chopped fresh parsley, if desired.
10. Serve the hot BBQ chicken wings immediately.

Nutritional Information (per serving):

- Calories: 320
- Protein: 24g
- Total Fats: 18g
- Fiber: 1g
- Carbohydrates: 14g

Spring Rolls

Time to Prepare: 20 minutes
Cooking Time: 10 minutes
Number of Servings: 4

Ingredients:

- 8 spring roll wrappers

- 1 cup of shredded cabbage
- 1 cup of shredded carrots
- 1 cup of bean sprouts
- 1/2 cup of chopped green onions
- 1/2 cup of chopped cilantro
- 1 tablespoon soy sauce
- 1 teaspoon of sesame oil
- 1 teaspoon of grated ginger
- 1 teaspoon of minced garlic
- 1 tablespoon cornstarch mixed with 2 tablespoons water (as a sealing agent)
- Cooking spray

Instructions List:

1. In a large mixing bowl, combine the shredded cabbage, carrots, bean sprouts, green onions, cilantro, soy sauce, sesame oil, ginger, and garlic. Mix well to combine.
2. Place a spring roll wrapper on a clean, flat surface with one corner facing you. Spoon about 2 tablespoons of the vegetable filling onto the bottom corner of the wrapper.
3. Fold the bottom corner of the wrapper over the filling, then fold in the side corners, and roll tightly to enclose the filling. Seal the edge with the cornstarch-water mixture.
4. Repeat the process with the remaining wrappers and filling.
5. Preheat your Ninja Foodi Digital Air Fryer Oven to 375°F on the Air Fry setting.
6. Lightly coat the air fryer basket or tray with cooking spray.
7. Arrange the prepared spring rolls in a single layer in the air fryer basket or on the air fryer tray, leaving some space between each roll.
8. Lightly spray the tops of the spring rolls with cooking spray.
9. Air fry the spring rolls at 375°F for 8-10 minutes, or until golden brown and crispy, flipping halfway through the cooking time.
10. Once done, remove the air-fried spring rolls from the air fryer and serve hot with your favorite dipping sauce.

Nutritional Information (per serving):

- Calories: 180
- Protein: 4g
- Total Fats: 3g
- Fiber: 2g
- Carbohydrates: 34g

Crispy Chickpeas

Time to Prepare: 5 minutes
Cooking Time: 15 minutes
Number of Servings: 4

Ingredients:

- 2 cans (15 ounces each) chickpeas, drained, rinsed, and patted dry
- 2 tablespoons olive oil
- 1 teaspoon of ground cumin
- 1 teaspoon of paprika
- 1/2 teaspoon of garlic powder
- 1/2 teaspoon of salt
- 1/4 teaspoon of black pepper

Instructions List:

1. Preheat your Ninja Foodi Digital Air Fryer Oven to 375°F on the Air Fry setting.
2. In a mixing bowl, combine the chickpeas, olive oil, ground cumin, paprika, garlic powder, salt, and black pepper. Toss until the chickpeas are evenly coated.
3. Spread the seasoned chickpeas in a single layer on the air fryer basket.
4. Air fry at 375°F for 15 minutes, shaking the basket halfway through the cooking time to ensure even cooking.
5. Once the chickpeas are crispy and golden brown, remove them from the air fryer.
6. Let the chickpeas cool slightly before serving.

7. Enjoy as a crunchy snack or use them as a topping for salads or soups!

Nutritional Information (per serving):

- Calories: 180
- Protein: 7g
- Total Fats: 7g
- Fiber: 6g
- Carbohydrates: 24g

Bacon-Wrapped Jalapeño Poppers

Time to Prepare: 20 minutes
Cooking Time: 10 minutes
Number of Servings: 6

Ingredients:

- 12 fresh jalapeño peppers
- 8 ounces cream cheese, softened
- 1 cup of shredded cheddar cheese
- 12 slices bacon

Instructions List:

1. Preheat your Ninja Foodi Digital Air Fryer Oven to 375°F on the Air Fry setting.
2. Cut the jalapeño peppers in half lengthwise and remove the seeds and membranes.
3. In a bowl, mix the softened cream cheese and shredded cheddar cheese until well fat.
4. Fill each jalapeño half with the cheese mixture.
5. Wrap each stuffed jalapeño half with a slice of bacon.
6. Place the bacon-wrapped jalapeño poppers in the air fryer basket in a single layer.
7. Air fry at 375°F for 10 minutes or until the bacon is crispy and the peppers are tender.
8. Once done, remove the bacon-wrapped jalapeño poppers from the air fryer.
9. Let them cool slightly before serving.
10. Enjoy your delicious bacon-wrapped jalapeño poppers as an appetizer or snack!

Nutritional Information (per serving):

- Calories: 284
- Protein: 10g
- Total Fats: 23g
- Fiber: 1g
- Carbohydrates: 6g

Mac and Cheese Bites

Time to Prepare: 20 minutes
Cooking Time: 15 minutes
Number of Servings: 6

Ingredients:

- 2 cups of cooked macaroni
- 1 cup of shredded cheddar cheese
- 1/2 cup of grated Parmesan cheese
- 1/4 cup of milk
- 1 large egg
- 1/2 teaspoon of garlic powder
- 1/2 teaspoon of onion powder
- Salt and pepper to taste
- 1 cup of breadcrumbs
- Cooking spray

Instructions List:

1. Preheat your Ninja Foodi Digital Air Fryer Oven to 375°F on the Bake setting.
2. In a large bowl, mix together the cooked macaroni, shredded cheddar cheese, grated Parmesan cheese, milk, egg, garlic powder, onion powder, salt, and pepper until well fat.
3. Using a spoon or cookie scoop, portion out the mac and cheese mixture and shape it into bite-sized balls.
4. Place the breadcrumbs on a plate.
5. Roll each mac and cheese ball in the breadcrumbs until fully coated.
6. Place the coated mac and cheese bites on a baking sheet or air fryer basket lined with parchment paper.

7. Lightly spray the mac and cheese bites with cooking spray.
8. Bake at 375°F for 15 minutes or until the bites are golden brown and crispy on the outside.
9. Once done, remove the mac and cheese bites from the air fryer.
10. Serve hot with your favorite dipping sauce.
11. Enjoy these delicious and cheesy mac and cheese bites!

Nutritional Information (per serving):

- Calories: 283
- Protein: 12g
- Total Fats: 12g
- Fiber: 2g
- Carbohydrates: 31g

Chapter 6: Vegetarian

Tofu Nuggets

Time to Prepare: 15 minutes
Cooking Time: 20 minutes
Number of Servings: 4

Ingredients:

- 1 block firm tofu, drained and pressed
- 1/2 cup of all-purpose flour
- 1 teaspoon of garlic powder
- 1 teaspoon of onion powder
- 1/2 teaspoon of paprika
- 1/2 teaspoon of salt
- 1/4 teaspoon of black pepper
- 2/3 cup unsweetened almond milk
- 1 cup of panko breadcrumbs
- Cooking spray

Instructions List:

1. Preheat your Ninja Foodi Digital Air Fryer Oven to 375°F.
2. Cut the pressed tofu into nugget-sized pieces.
3. In a shallow bowl, mix the all-purpose flour, garlic powder, onion powder, paprika, salt, and black pepper.
4. In another shallow bowl, pour the unsweetened almond milk.
5. Place the panko breadcrumbs in a third shallow bowl.
6. Dredge each tofu piece in the flour mixture, then dip into the almond milk, and finally coat with panko breadcrumbs.
7. Arrange the breaded tofu nuggets in a single layer in the air fryer basket, ensuring they do not touch each other.
8. Lightly spray the tofu nuggets with cooking spray.
9. Air fry at 375°F for 20 minutes, flipping halfway through the cooking time until the nuggets are golden brown and crispy.
10. Serve the tofu nuggets hot with your favorite dipping sauce.
11. Enjoy these crispy and delicious air-fried tofu nuggets!

Nutritional Information (per serving):

- Calories: 230
- Protein: 12g
- Total Fats: 8g
- Fiber: 2g
- Carbohydrates: 27g

Stuffed Bell Peppers

Time to Prepare: 15 minutes
Cooking Time: 30 minutes
Number of Servings: 4

Ingredients:

- 4 large bell peppers, tops cut off and seeds removed
- 1 lb ground beef
- 1 cup of cooked rice
- 1 small onion, finely chopped
- 2 cloves garlic, minced
- 1 can (15 oz) diced tomatoes, drained
- 1 cup of shredded cheddar cheese
- 1 teaspoon of dried oregano
- 1 teaspoon of dried basil
- Salt and pepper to taste
- Cooking spray

Instructions List:

1. Preheat your Ninja Foodi Digital Air Fryer Oven to 375°F.
2. In a large skillet, cook the ground beef over medium heat until browned. Drain any excess fat.

3. Add the onion and garlic to the skillet, cooking until softened, about 5 minutes.
4. Stir in the cooked rice, diced tomatoes, oregano, basil, salt, and pepper. Cook for an additional 2 minutes.
5. Spoon the beef mixture evenly into each bell pepper.
6. Place the stuffed peppers in a baking dish that fits in your Ninja Foodi Digital Air Fryer Oven.
7. Sprinkle the shredded cheddar cheese on top of each stuffed pepper.
8. Lightly spray the stuffed peppers with cooking spray.
9. Bake at 375°F for 30 minutes, until the peppers are tender and the cheese is melted and bubbly.
10. Serve the stuffed bell peppers hot and enjoy.

Nutritional Information (per serving):

- Calories: 380
- Protein: 28g
- Total Fats: 20g
- Fiber: 5g
- Carbohydrates: 25g

Cauliflower Buffalo Wings

Time to Prepare: 15 minutes
Cooking Time: 25 minutes
Number of Servings: 4

Ingredients:

- 1 large head of cauliflower, cut into bite-sized florets
- 1 cup of all-purpose flour
- 1 teaspoon of garlic powder
- 1 teaspoon of onion powder
- 1 teaspoon of paprika
- 1/2 teaspoon of salt
- 1/2 teaspoon of black pepper
- 1 cup of water
- 1 cup of buffalo sauce
- Cooking spray

Instructions List:

1. Preheat your Ninja Foodi Digital Air Fryer Oven to 400°F.
2. In a large bowl, combine flour, garlic powder, onion powder, paprika, salt, and black pepper.
3. Add water to the bowl and whisk until a smooth batter forms.
4. Dip each cauliflower floret into the batter, allowing any excess to drip off.
5. Place the battered cauliflower florets in the air fryer basket in a single layer, making sure they are not touching.
6. Lightly spray the cauliflower with cooking spray.
7. Air fry at 400°F for 20 minutes, shaking the basket halfway through the cooking time.
8. In a small bowl, toss the air-fried cauliflower florets with the buffalo sauce until evenly coated.
9. Return the coated cauliflower to the air fryer and air fry for an additional 5 minutes.
10. Serve the cauliflower buffalo wings hot, with your favorite dipping sauce.

Nutritional Information (per serving):

- Calories: 190
- Protein: 5g
- Total Fats: 2g
- Fiber: 4g
- Carbohydrates: 35g

Eggplant Parmesan

Time to Prepare: 20 minutes
Cooking Time: 25 minutes
Number of Servings: 4

Ingredients:

- 1 large eggplant, sliced into 1/4-inch rounds

- 1 cup of all-purpose flour
- 2 large eggs, beaten
- 1 cup of panko breadcrumbs
- 1/2 cup of grated Parmesan cheese
- 1 teaspoon of garlic powder
- 1 teaspoon of dried oregano
- 1/2 teaspoon of salt
- 1/2 teaspoon of black pepper
- Cooking spray
- 1 cup of marinara sauce
- 1 cup of shredded mozzarella cheese
- Fresh basil leaves for garnish (optional)

Instructions List:

1. Preheat your Ninja Foodi Digital Air Fryer Oven to 375°F.
2. Set up a breading station with three shallow bowls. Place flour in the first bowl, beaten eggs in the second bowl, and a mixture of panko breadcrumbs, grated Parmesan cheese, garlic powder, dried oregano, salt, and black pepper in the third bowl.
3. Dip each eggplant slice into the flour, shaking off any excess. Then dip into the beaten eggs, and finally coat with the breadcrumb mixture, pressing lightly to adhere.
4. Place the breaded eggplant slices in a single layer in the air fryer basket. Lightly spray with cooking spray.
5. Air fry at 375°F for 15 minutes, flipping halfway through, until the eggplant is golden brown and crispy.
6. Remove the eggplant slices from the air fryer and spread a thin layer of marinara sauce over each slice. Sprinkle shredded mozzarella cheese on top.
7. Return the eggplant slices to the air fryer and air fry at 375°F for an additional 5-7 minutes, or until the cheese is melted and bubbly.
8. Garnish with fresh basil leaves if desired, and serve hot.

Nutritional Information (per serving):

- Calories: 310
- Protein: 15g
- Total Fats: 12g
- Fiber: 6g
- Carbohydrates: 38g

Quinoa-Stuffed Portobello Mushrooms

Time to Prepare: 20 minutes
Cooking Time: 25 minutes
Number of Servings: 4

Ingredients:

- 4 large Portobello mushrooms, stems removed and gills scraped
- 1 cup of cooked quinoa
- 1/2 cup of cherry tomatoes, diced
- 1/2 cup of spinach, chopped
- 1/4 cup of feta cheese, crumbled
- 1/4 cup of grated Parmesan cheese
- 2 tablespoons olive oil
- 1 garlic clove, minced
- 1 teaspoon of dried oregano
- 1 teaspoon of salt
- 1/2 teaspoon of black pepper

Instructions List:

1. Preheat your Ninja Foodi Digital Air Fryer Oven to 375°F.
2. In a large bowl, combine cooked quinoa, cherry tomatoes, spinach, feta cheese, Parmesan cheese, minced garlic, dried oregano, salt, and black pepper. Mix well.
3. Brush the Portobello mushroom caps with olive oil on both sides.
4. Place the mushrooms on a baking tray and fill each mushroom cap with the quinoa mixture, pressing gently to pack the filling.

5. Bake at 375°F for 20-25 minutes, until the mushrooms are tender and the filling is heated through and slightly golden on top.
6. Serve immediately.

Nutritional Information (per serving):

- Calories: 210
- Protein: 7g
- Total Fats: 12g
- Fiber: 3g
- Carbohydrates: 19g

Falafel

Time to Prepare: 15 minutes
Cooking Time: 15 minutes
Number of Servings: 4

Ingredients:

- 1 can (15 oz) chickpeas, drained and rinsed
- 1/2 cup of fresh parsley, chopped
- 1/4 cup of fresh cilantro, chopped
- 1 small onion, finely chopped
- 2 garlic cloves, minced
- 1 teaspoon of ground cumin
- 1 teaspoon of ground coriander
- 1/2 teaspoon of baking powder
- 1/2 teaspoon of salt
- 1/4 teaspoon of black pepper
- 3 tablespoons all-purpose flour
- 2 tablespoons olive oil

Instructions List:

1. Preheat your Ninja Foodi Digital Air Fryer Oven to 375°F.
2. In a food processor, combine chickpeas, parsley, cilantro, onion, garlic, cumin, coriander, baking powder, salt, and black pepper. Pulse until well fat but still slightly chunky.
3. Transfer the mixture to a bowl and stir in the flour until well fat.
4. Form the mixture into small balls or patties, about 1-2 tablespoons each.
5. Brush or spray the falafel balls with olive oil.
6. Place the falafel balls in the air fryer basket in a single layer, leaving space between them.
7. Air fry at 375°F for 12-15 minutes, turning halfway through, until golden brown and crispy.
8. Serve immediately.

Nutritional Information (per serving):

- Calories: 180
- Protein: 6g
- Total Fats: 8g
- Fiber: 5g
- Carbohydrates: 22g

Veggie Stir-Fry with Tofu

Time to Prepare: 15 minutes
Cooking Time: 10 minutes
Number of Servings: 4

Ingredients:

- 1 block (14 oz) firm tofu, drained and cubed
- 2 tablespoons soy sauce
- 1 tablespoon sesame oil
- 1 tablespoon olive oil
- 1 red bell pepper, sliced
- 1 yellow bell pepper, sliced
- 1 cup of broccoli florets
- 1 cup of snap peas
- 1 carrot, julienned
- 3 garlic cloves, minced
- 1 tablespoon fresh ginger, minced
- 2 green onions, chopped
- 1 tablespoon sesame seeds

- Salt and pepper to taste

Instructions List:

1. Preheat your Ninja Foodi Digital Air Fryer Oven to 400°F.
2. In a bowl, toss the tofu cubes with soy sauce and sesame oil.
3. Arrange the tofu cubes on a baking sheet lined with parchment paper.
4. Broil the tofu for 5 minutes, turning once halfway through, until golden brown.
5. In a large bowl, combine the bell peppers, broccoli, snap peas, and carrot with olive oil, garlic, and ginger. Toss to coat evenly.
6. Spread the vegetable mixture on another baking sheet lined with parchment paper.
7. Broil the vegetables for 5 minutes, stirring once halfway through, until tender-crisp.
8. Combine the broiled tofu and vegetables in a serving dish, sprinkle with green onions and sesame seeds.
9. Season with salt and pepper to taste. Serve immediately.

Nutritional Information (per serving):

- Calories: 210
- Protein: 10g
- Total Fats: 12g
- Fiber: 4g
- Carbohydrates: 16g

Crispy Brussels Sprouts

Time to Prepare: 10 minutes
Cooking Time: 15 minutes
Number of Servings: 4

Ingredients:

- 1 lb Brussels sprouts, trimmed and halved
- 2 tablespoons olive oil
- 1 teaspoon of garlic powder
- 1 teaspoon of smoked paprika
- Salt and pepper to taste
- 2 tablespoons grated Parmesan cheese (optional)

Instructions List:

1. Preheat your Ninja Foodi Digital Air Fryer Oven to 375°F.
2. In a large bowl, toss the Brussels sprouts with olive oil, garlic powder, smoked paprika, salt, and pepper until evenly coated.
3. Place the Brussels sprouts in a single layer in the air fryer basket.
4. Air fry for 15 minutes, shaking the basket halfway through to ensure even cooking.
5. Remove from the air fryer and sprinkle with grated Parmesan cheese, if desired.
6. Serve immediately.

Nutritional Information (per serving):

- Calories: 110
- Protein: 3g
- Total Fats: 7g
- Fiber: 4g
- Carbohydrates: 10g

Stuffed Artichokes

Time to Prepare: 20 minutes
Cooking Time: 25 minutes
Number of Servings: 4

Ingredients:

- 4 medium artichokes, trimmed and cleaned
- 1 cup of breadcrumbs
- 1/2 cup of grated Parmesan cheese
- 1/4 cup of chopped fresh parsley
- 3 cloves garlic, minced
- 1/4 cup of olive oil
- Juice of 1 lemon
- Salt and pepper to taste

Instructions List:

1. Preheat your Ninja Foodi Digital Air Fryer Oven to 350°F.
2. In a large bowl, combine breadcrumbs, Parmesan cheese, parsley, and minced garlic.
3. Drizzle the mixture with olive oil and lemon juice, then season with salt and pepper. Mix well.
4. Stuff each artichoke with the breadcrumb mixture, pressing it between the leaves.
5. Place the stuffed artichokes in the air fryer basket.
6. Air fry for 25 minutes, or until the artichokes are tender and the stuffing is golden brown.
7. Serve immediately.

Nutritional Information (per serving):

- Calories: 230
- Protein: 7g
- Total Fats: 12g
- Fiber: 9g
- Carbohydrates: 24g

Ratatouille

Time to Prepare: 20 minutes
Cooking Time: 25 minutes
Number of Servings: 4

Ingredients:

- 1 medium eggplant, diced
- 2 medium zucchinis, diced
- 1 large red bell pepper, diced
- 1 large yellow bell pepper, diced
- 1 onion, diced
- 3 cloves garlic, minced
- 2 tablespoons olive oil
- 1 teaspoon of dried thyme
- 1 teaspoon of dried oregano
- Salt and pepper to taste
- 1 can (14 oz) diced tomatoes
- Fresh basil leaves, chopped (for garnish)

Instructions List:

1. Preheat your Ninja Foodi Digital Air Fryer Oven to 375°F.
2. In a large bowl, toss the diced eggplant, zucchinis, bell peppers, onion, and garlic with olive oil, thyme, oregano, salt, and pepper until evenly coated.
3. Spread the seasoned vegetables in a single layer on the air fryer basket.
4. Air fry for 20-25 minutes, shaking the basket halfway through, until the vegetables are tender and slightly caramelized.
5. Transfer the cooked vegetables to a serving dish and stir in the diced tomatoes.
6. Garnish with chopped fresh basil leaves before serving.

Nutritional Information (per serving):

- Calories: 150
- Protein: 3g
- Total Fats: 7g
- Fiber: 7g
- Carbohydrates: 21g

Veggie Burgers

Time to Prepare: 15 minutes
Cooking Time: 15 minutes
Number of Servings: 4

Ingredients:

- 2 cups of cooked quinoa
- 1 can (15 oz) black beans, drained and rinsed
- 1 cup of breadcrumbs
- 1/2 cup of grated carrots
- 1/4 cup of chopped red bell pepper
- 1/4 cup of chopped green onions
- 2 cloves garlic, minced
- 2 tablespoons soy sauce

- 1 teaspoon of ground cumin
- 1 teaspoon of chili powder
- Salt and pepper to taste
- Cooking spray

Instructions List:

1. In a large mixing bowl, mash the black beans using a fork or potato masher.
2. Add the cooked quinoa, breadcrumbs, grated carrots, chopped red bell pepper, chopped green onions, minced garlic, soy sauce, ground cumin, chili powder, salt, and pepper to the bowl. Mix until well fat.
3. Divide the mixture into 4 equal portions and shape each portion into a patty.
4. Preheat your Ninja Foodi Digital Air Fryer Oven to 375°F.
5. Lightly coat the air fryer basket with cooking spray.
6. Place the veggie burger patties in the air fryer basket, leaving space between each patty.
7. Air fry for 15 minutes, flipping halfway through the cooking time, until the patties are golden brown and crispy on the outside.
8. Once done, remove the veggie burgers from the air fryer and serve immediately, either on buns with your favorite toppings or alongside a salad.

Nutritional Information (per serving):

- Calories: 280
- Protein: 10g
- Total Fats: 4g
- Fiber: 8g
- Carbohydrates: 50g

Spicy Roasted Chickpeas

Time to Prepare: 10 minutes
Cooking Time: 20 minutes
Number of Servings: 4

Ingredients:

- 2 cans (15 ounces each) chickpeas, drained, rinsed, and patted dry
- 2 tablespoons olive oil
- 1 teaspoon of ground cumin
- 1 teaspoon of paprika
- 1/2 teaspoon of garlic powder
- 1/2 teaspoon of onion powder
- 1/4 teaspoon of cayenne pepper (adjust to taste)
- Salt to taste

Instructions List:

1. Preheat your Ninja Foodi Digital Air Fryer Oven to 400°F.
2. In a mixing bowl, combine the chickpeas, olive oil, ground cumin, paprika, garlic powder, onion powder, cayenne pepper, and salt. Toss until the chickpeas are evenly coated with the spices.
3. Spread the seasoned chickpeas in a single layer on the air fryer basket.
4. Air fry the chickpeas at 400°F for 20 minutes, shaking the basket halfway through the cooking time.
5. Once done, remove the chickpeas from the air fryer and let them cool slightly before serving.
6. Enjoy the spicy roasted chickpeas as a crunchy snack or as a topping for salads and soups.

Nutritional Information (per serving):

- Calories: 210
- Protein: 7g
- Total Fats: 8g
- Fiber: 7g
- Carbohydrates: 29g

Stuffed Zucchini Boats

Time to Prepare: 15 minutes
Cooking Time: 20 minutes
Number of Servings: 4

Ingredients:

- 2 large zucchinis
- 1/2 cup of marinara sauce
- 1/2 cup of shredded mozzarella cheese
- 1/4 cup of grated Parmesan cheese
- 1/4 cup of chopped fresh basil
- 1/4 teaspoon of garlic powder
- Salt and pepper to taste
- Olive oil spray

Instructions List:

1. Preheat your Ninja Foodi Digital Air Fryer Oven to 375°F.
2. Cut the zucchinis in half lengthwise and scoop out the seeds to form boats.
3. In a bowl, mix together the marinara sauce, shredded mozzarella cheese, grated Parmesan cheese, chopped fresh basil, garlic powder, salt, and pepper.
4. Stuff each zucchini boat with the filling mixture.
5. Lightly spray the air fryer basket with olive oil spray.
6. Place the stuffed zucchini boats in the air fryer basket.
7. Air fry at 375°F for 20 minutes or until the zucchinis are tender and the cheese is melted and bubbly.
8. Serve hot and enjoy!

Nutritional Information (per serving):

- Calories: 110
- Protein: 7g
- Total Fats: 7g
- Fiber: 3g
- Carbohydrates: 7g

Chapter 7: Desserts

Apple Fritters

Time to Prepare: 15 minutes
Cooking Time: 10 minutes
Number of Servings: 4

Ingredients:

- 2 cups of all-purpose flour
- 1/4 cup of granulated sugar
- 2 teaspoons of baking powder
- 1/2 teaspoon of ground cinnamon
- 1/4 teaspoon of salt
- 2 large eggs
- 1/2 cup of milk
- 2 tablespoons unsalted butter, melted
- 2 medium apples, peeled, cored, and diced
- Vegetable oil spray
- Powdered sugar, for dusting (optional)

Instructions List:

1. Preheat your Ninja Foodi Digital Air Fryer Oven to 350°F.
2. In a large bowl, whisk together the flour, sugar, baking powder, cinnamon, and salt.
3. In another bowl, beat the eggs, then add the milk and melted butter, and mix until well fat.
4. Pour the wet ingredients into the dry ingredients and stir until just fat. Do not overmix.
5. Fold in the diced apples until evenly distributed throughout the batter.
6. Lightly spray the air fryer basket with vegetable oil spray.
7. Drop spoonfuls of the batter into the air fryer basket, leaving space between each fritter.
8. Air fry at 350°F for 8-10 minutes or until the fritters are golden brown and cooked through.
9. Remove the fritters from the air fryer and let them cool slightly.
10. Dust with powdered sugar, if desired, and serve warm.

Nutritional Information (per serving):

- Calories: 260
- Protein: 6g
- Total Fats: 7g
- Fiber: 2g
- Carbohydrates: 44g

Chocolate Lava Cake

Time to Prepare: 15 minutes
Cooking Time: 12 minutes
Number of Servings: 4

Ingredients:

- 1/2 cup of (1 stick) unsalted butter
- 4 ounces semi-sweet chocolate, chopped
- 2 large eggs
- 2 large egg yolks
- 1/4 cup of granulated sugar
- 2 tablespoons all-purpose flour
- Pinch of salt
- Powdered sugar, for dusting (optional)
- Fresh berries, for garnish (optional)
- Vanilla ice cream, for serving (optional)

Instructions List:

1. Preheat your Ninja Foodi Digital Air Fryer Oven to 375°F.
2. In a microwave-safe bowl, combine the butter and chopped chocolate. Microwave in 30-second intervals, stirring in between, until melted and smooth. Set aside to cool slightly.

3. In a separate bowl, whisk together the eggs, egg yolks, and granulated sugar until pale and fluffy.
4. Slowly pour the melted chocolate mixture into the egg mixture, whisking constantly, until well fat.
5. Sift in the flour and add the salt. Gently fold until just fat, being careful not to overmix.
6. Lightly grease four ramekins with butter or cooking spray.
7. Divide the batter evenly among the prepared ramekins.
8. Place the ramekins in the air fryer basket or on the air fryer tray.
9. Air fry at 375°F for 12 minutes or until the edges are set but the centers are still slightly jiggly.
10. Carefully remove the ramekins from the air fryer and let them cool for a few minutes.
11. Run a knife around the edges of each cake to loosen them, then invert them onto serving plates.
12. Dust with powdered sugar, if desired, and garnish with fresh berries.
13. Serve warm with vanilla ice cream, if desired.

Nutritional Information (per serving):

- Calories: 410
- Protein: 6g
- Total Fats: 30g
- Fiber: 2g
- Carbohydrates: 32g

Lemon Blueberry Scones

Time to Prepare: 15 minutes
Cooking Time: 15 minutes
Number of Servings: 8

Ingredients:

- 2 cups of all-purpose flour
- 1/3 cup granulated sugar
- 1 tablespoon baking powder
- 1/2 teaspoon of salt
- Zest of 1 lemon
- 1/2 cup of unsalted butter, cold and cubed
- 1/2 cup of heavy cream
- 1 large egg
- 1 teaspoon of vanilla extract
- 1 cup of fresh blueberries

Instructions List:

1. Preheat your Ninja Foodi Digital Air Fryer Oven to 375°F.
2. In a large mixing bowl, whisk together the flour, sugar, baking powder, salt, and lemon zest.
3. Add the cold cubed butter to the dry ingredients. Using a pastry cutter or your fingers, work the butter into the flour mixture until it resembles coarse crumbs.
4. In a separate bowl, whisk together the heavy cream, egg, and vanilla extract.
5. Pour the wet ingredients into the dry ingredients and stir until just fat.
6. Gently fold in the fresh blueberries.
7. Turn the dough out onto a lightly floured surface and shape it into a circle about 1-inch thick.
8. Cut the dough into 8 equal wedges.
9. Place the scones on a parchment-lined baking sheet or in the air fryer basket, leaving space between each one.
10. Bake at 375°F for 15 minutes or until the scones are golden brown and cooked through.
11. Remove from the oven and let cool slightly before serving.

Nutritional Information (per serving):

- Calories: 260
- Protein: 4g
- Total Fats: 14g

- Fiber: 1g
- Carbohydrates: 31g

Peanut Butter Cookies

Time to Prepare: 15 minutes
Cooking Time: 10 minutes
Number of Servings: 12 cookies

Ingredients:

- 1 cup of peanut butter
- 1/2 cup of granulated sugar
- 1/2 cup of packed brown sugar
- 1 large egg
- 1 teaspoon of vanilla extract

Instructions List:

1. Preheat your Ninja Foodi Digital Air Fryer Oven to 350°F.
2. In a large mixing bowl, combine peanut butter, granulated sugar, brown sugar, egg, and vanilla extract. Mix until well fat.
3. Shape the dough into 1-inch balls and place them on a parchment-lined air fryer basket or tray, spacing them about 2 inches apart.
4. Use a fork to gently flatten each cookie, creating a crisscross pattern on top.
5. Place the cookies in the preheated air fryer oven and bake for 10 minutes, or until the edges are golden brown.
6. Remove the cookies from the air fryer and let them cool on a wire rack before serving.

Nutritional Information (per serving):

- Calories: 200
- Protein: 5g
- Total Fats: 13g
- Fiber: 2g
- Carbohydrates: 18g

Donuts

Time to Prepare: 20 minutes
Cooking Time: 10 minutes
Number of Servings: 6 donuts

Ingredients:

- 1 can refrigerated biscuit dough (8-count)
- 1/4 cup of granulated sugar
- 1 teaspoon of ground cinnamon
- 2 tablespoons melted butter

Instructions List:

1. Preheat your Ninja Foodi Digital Air Fryer Oven to 350°F.
2. Remove the biscuit dough from the can and separate into individual biscuits.
3. Use a small round cookie cutter or the back of a piping tip to cut a hole in the center of each biscuit to form the donuts.
4. In a small bowl, mix together granulated sugar and ground cinnamon.
5. Lightly brush both sides of each biscuit with melted butter, then dip them into the cinnamon-sugar mixture, coating evenly.
6. Place the coated biscuits on the air fryer basket or tray in a single layer, leaving space between each donut.
7. Air fry the donuts at 350°F for 5 minutes, then flip them over and air fry for another 5 minutes, or until golden brown and cooked through.
8. Remove the donuts from the air fryer and let them cool slightly before serving.

Nutritional Information (per serving):

- Calories: 190
- Protein: 2g
- Total Fats: 10g
- Fiber: 1g
- Carbohydrates: 23g

Cinnamon Sugar Pretzel Bites

Time to Prepare: 30 minutes
Cooking Time: 10 minutes
Number of Servings: 4 servings

Ingredients:

- 1 can refrigerated pizza dough
- 2 tablespoons baking soda
- 2 cups of water
- 2 tablespoons melted butter
- 1/4 cup of granulated sugar
- 1 teaspoon of ground cinnamon

Instructions List:

1. Preheat your Ninja Foodi Digital Air Fryer Oven to 350°F.
2. Roll out the pizza dough on a lightly floured surface into a rectangle, about 1/4 inch thick.
3. Cut the dough into small squares to form the pretzel bites.
4. In a saucepan, bring the water and baking soda to a boil. Drop the pretzel bites into the boiling water in batches for about 20 seconds, then remove them with a slotted spoon and place them on a paper towel-lined plate to drain excess water.
5. Place the drained pretzel bites on the air fryer basket or tray in a single layer, leaving space between each bite.
6. Air fry the pretzel bites at 350°F for 8-10 minutes, or until golden brown and crispy.
7. In a small bowl, mix together granulated sugar and ground cinnamon.
8. Brush the melted butter over the hot pretzel bites, then toss them in the cinnamon sugar mixture until coated evenly.
9. Serve the cinnamon sugar pretzel bites warm.

Nutritional Information (per serving):

- Calories: 280
- Protein: 4g
- Total Fats: 8g
- Fiber: 1g
- Carbohydrates: 47g

Raspberry Cheesecake Bites

Time to Prepare: 20 minutes
Cooking Time: 25 minutes
Number of Servings: 12 bites

Ingredients:

- 1 cup of graham cracker crumbs
- 2 tablespoons melted butter
- 8 ounces cream cheese, softened
- 1/4 cup of granulated sugar
- 1 egg
- 1 teaspoon of vanilla extract
- 1/2 cup of raspberry jam
- Fresh raspberries for garnish (optional)

Instructions List:

1. Preheat your Ninja Foodi Digital Air Fryer Oven to 325°F.
2. In a mixing bowl, combine the graham cracker crumbs and melted butter until the mixture resembles wet sand.
3. Press the graham cracker mixture firmly into the bottom of a lined and greased muffin tin to form the crust for the cheesecake bites.
4. In another bowl, beat the cream cheese, granulated sugar, egg, and vanilla extract until smooth and creamy.
5. Spoon the cream cheese mixture over the graham cracker crust in the muffin tin, filling each cup about two-thirds full.
6. Drop small spoonfuls of raspberry jam on top of the cream cheese mixture in each cup.
7. Using a toothpick or skewer, swirl the raspberry jam into the cream cheese mixture to create a marbled effect.
8. Place the muffin tin in the air fryer basket or on the air fryer tray.

9. Air fry the cheesecake bites at 325°F for 20-25 minutes, or until the edges are set and the centers are slightly jiggly.
10. Remove the cheesecake bites from the air fryer and allow them to cool in the muffin tin for 10 minutes.
11. Transfer the cheesecake bites to a wire rack to cool completely.
12. Once cooled, garnish each cheesecake bite with a fresh raspberry if desired.
13. Chill the cheesecake bites in the refrigerator for at least 1 hour before serving.

Nutritional Information (per serving):

- Calories: 180
- Protein: 2g
- Total Fats: 11g
- Fiber: 1g
- Carbohydrates: 19g

Pineapple Upside-Down Cake

Time to Prepare: 20 minutes
Cooking Time: 30 minutes
Servings: 8

Ingredients:

- 1/4 cup of unsalted butter, melted
- 1/2 cup of packed brown sugar
- 1 can (20 oz) pineapple slices, drained
- 1 jar (6 oz) maraschino cherries, drained
- 1 box yellow cake mix
- 3 large eggs
- 1/3 cup vegetable oil
- 1 cup of water

Instructions List:

1. Preheat the Ninja Foodi Digital Air Fryer Oven to 350°F.
2. In a small bowl, mix melted butter and brown sugar until well fat.
3. Spread the butter-sugar mixture evenly on the bottom of the air fryer basket.
4. Arrange pineapple slices and maraschino cherries on top of the sugar mixture in a decorative pattern.
5. In a large bowl, combine cake mix, eggs, vegetable oil, and water. Mix until smooth.
6. Pour the cake batter over the pineapple and cherries, spreading it evenly.
7. Place the air fryer basket in the oven and bake for 30 minutes, or until a toothpick inserted into the center comes out clean.
8. Once done, remove the cake from the oven and let it cool in the basket for 10 minutes.
9. Carefully invert the cake onto a serving plate. Serve warm or at room temperature.

Nutritional Information (per serving):

- Calories: 385
- Protein: 3g
- Total Fats: 16g
- Fiber: 1g
- Carbohydrates: 58g

Brownies

Time to Prepare: 15 minutes
Cooking Time: 20 minutes
Servings: 12

Ingredients:

- 1/2 cup of unsalted butter
- 1 cup of granulated sugar
- 2 large eggs
- 1 teaspoon of vanilla extract
- 1/3 cup unsweetened cocoa powder
- 1/2 cup of all-purpose flour
- 1/4 teaspoon of salt
- 1/4 teaspoon of baking powder
- 1/2 cup of chocolate chips

Instructions List:

1. Preheat the Ninja Foodi Digital Air Fryer Oven to 325°F.
2. Grease a square baking pan that fits inside the air fryer basket.
3. In a microwave-safe bowl, melt the butter in the microwave.
4. Once melted, stir in the sugar until well fat.
5. Add the eggs and vanilla extract to the butter-sugar mixture. Mix until smooth.
6. Sift in cocoa powder, flour, salt, and baking powder. Mix until just fat.
7. Fold in the chocolate chips.
8. Pour the batter into the prepared baking pan and smooth the top.
9. Place the baking pan in the air fryer basket and insert it into the oven.
10. Air fry the brownies at 325°F for 20 minutes, or until a toothpick inserted into the center comes out with a few moist crumbs.
11. Once done, remove the baking pan from the air fryer and let the brownies cool before slicing.

Nutritional Information (per serving):

- Calories: 210
- Protein: 3g
- Total Fats: 12g
- Fiber: 1g
- Carbohydrates: 26g

Oreos

Time to Prepare: 10 minutes
Cooking Time: 8 minutes
Servings: 4

Ingredients:

- 16 Oreo cookies
- 1 cup of pancake mix
- 1/2 cup of milk
- 1 large egg
- 1 teaspoon of vanilla extract
- Powdered sugar, for dusting (optional)

Instructions List:

1. Preheat the Ninja Foodi Digital Air Fryer Oven to 350°F.
2. In a shallow bowl, whisk together pancake mix, milk, egg, and vanilla extract until smooth.
3. Dip each Oreo cookie into the pancake batter, coating it evenly.
4. Place the coated Oreos in the air fryer basket in a single layer, leaving space between each cookie.
5. Air fry the Oreos at 350°F for 8 minutes, or until they are golden brown and crispy.
6. Once done, remove the Oreos from the air fryer and let them cool for a few minutes.
7. Optionally, dust the air-fried Oreos with powdered sugar before serving.

Nutritional Information (per serving):

- Calories: 300
- Protein: 5g
- Total Fats: 12g
- Fiber: 1g
- Carbohydrates: 45g

Chocolate Chip Muffins

Time to Prepare: 15 minutes
Cooking Time: 18 minutes
Servings: 12

Ingredients:

- 2 cups of all-purpose flour
- 1/2 cup of granulated sugar
- 1/4 cup of packed brown sugar
- 2 teaspoons of baking powder
- 1/2 teaspoon of baking soda
- 1/4 teaspoon of salt
- 1 cup of milk
- 1/2 cup of unsalted butter, melted

- 2 large eggs
- 1 teaspoon of vanilla extract
- 1 cup of semi-sweet chocolate chips

Instructions List:

1. Preheat the Ninja Foodi Digital Air Fryer Oven to 350°F.
2. In a large mixing bowl, whisk together flour, granulated sugar, brown sugar, baking powder, baking soda, and salt.
3. In a separate bowl, mix together milk, melted butter, eggs, and vanilla extract until well fat.
4. Pour the wet ingredients into the dry ingredients and stir until just fat.
5. Fold in the chocolate chips.
6. Line a muffin tin with paper liners or grease it with cooking spray.
7. Divide the muffin batter evenly among the muffin cups, filling each about two-thirds full.
8. Place the muffin tin in the air fryer basket and insert it into the oven.
9. Bake the muffins at 350°F for 18 minutes, or until a toothpick inserted into the center of a muffin comes out clean.
10. Once done, remove the muffins from the air fryer and let them cool for a few minutes before serving.

Nutritional Information (per serving):

- Calories: 280
- Protein: 4g
- Total Fats: 14g
- Fiber: 2g
- Carbohydrates: 36g

Peach Cobbler

Time to Prepare: 15 minutes
Cooking Time: 25 minutes
Servings: 6

Ingredients:

- 4 cups of sliced peaches (fresh or canned, drained)
- 1/4 cup of granulated sugar
- 1 tablespoon lemon juice
- 1 teaspoon of ground cinnamon
- 1/2 teaspoon of vanilla extract
- 1 cup of all-purpose flour
- 1/2 cup of granulated sugar
- 1 teaspoon of baking powder
- 1/4 teaspoon of salt
- 1/2 cup of unsalted butter, melted
- 1/2 cup of milk

Instructions List:

1. Preheat the Ninja Foodi Digital Air Fryer Oven to 375°F.
2. In a mixing bowl, combine sliced peaches, 1/4 cup of granulated sugar, lemon juice, cinnamon, and vanilla extract. Toss until the peaches are evenly coated.
3. In another bowl, whisk together flour, remaining 1/2 cup of granulated sugar, baking powder, and salt.
4. Stir in melted butter and milk into the flour mixture until just fat.
5. Spread the peach mixture evenly into the bottom of a greased air fryer-safe baking dish.
6. Drop spoonfuls of the batter over the peaches.
7. Place the baking dish in the air fryer basket and insert it into the oven.
8. Air fry the peach cobbler at 375°F for 25 minutes, or until the top is golden brown and the peaches are bubbly.
9. Once done, remove the cobbler from the air fryer and let it cool for a few minutes before serving.

Nutritional Information (per serving):

- Calories: 320
- Protein: 3g

- Total Fats: 13g
- Fiber: 3g
- Carbohydrates: 51g

Bread Pudding

Time to Prepare: 20 minutes
Cooking Time: 25 minutes
Servings: 6

Ingredients:

- 6 cups of cubed bread (such as French bread or brioche)
- 2 cups of whole milk
- 3 large eggs
- 1/2 cup of granulated sugar
- 1 teaspoon of vanilla extract
- 1/2 teaspoon of ground cinnamon
- 1/4 teaspoon of ground nutmeg
- 1/4 cup of raisins (optional)
- 2 tablespoons unsalted butter, melted

Instructions List:

1. Preheat the Ninja Foodi Digital Air Fryer Oven to 350°F.
2. In a large mixing bowl, combine cubed bread and milk. Let it sit for 10 minutes, allowing the bread to soak up the milk.
3. In another bowl, whisk together eggs, sugar, vanilla extract, cinnamon, and nutmeg until well fat.
4. Pour the egg mixture over the soaked bread and stir gently to combine. If desired, fold in raisins.
5. Grease a baking dish that fits inside the air fryer basket with melted butter.
6. Transfer the bread mixture into the prepared baking dish, spreading it evenly.
7. Place the baking dish in the air fryer basket and insert it into the oven.
8. Air fry the bread pudding at 350°F for 25 minutes, or until the top is golden brown and the pudding is set.
9. Once done, remove the bread pudding from the air fryer and let it cool for a few minutes before serving.

Nutritional Information (per serving):

- Calories: 300
- Protein: 8g
- Total Fats: 10g
- Fiber: 2g
- Carbohydrates: 45g

Strawberry Shortcake

Time to Prepare: 20 minutes
Cooking Time: 25 minutes
Servings: 6

Ingredients:

- 2 cups of all-purpose flour
- 1/4 cup of granulated sugar
- 1 tablespoon baking powder
- 1/2 teaspoon of salt
- 1/2 cup of unsalted butter, cold and cubed
- 2/3 cup milk
- 1 teaspoon of vanilla extract
- 2 cups of sliced strawberries
- 2 tablespoons granulated sugar
- Whipped cream, for serving

Instructions List:

1. Preheat the Ninja Foodi Digital Air Fryer Oven to 375°F.
2. In a large mixing bowl, combine flour, 1/4 cup of sugar, baking powder, and salt.
3. Add cold cubed butter to the flour mixture. Use a pastry cutter or fork to cut the butter into the flour until the mixture resembles coarse crumbs.

4. In a separate bowl, mix together milk and vanilla extract.
5. Pour the milk mixture into the flour mixture and stir until just fat.
6. Transfer the dough onto a lightly floured surface and gently knead a few times until it comes together.
7. Pat the dough into a circle about 1 inch thick. Use a round cutter to cut out 6 biscuits.
8. Place the biscuits on a parchment-lined baking sheet and bake in the air fryer for 20-25 minutes, or until golden brown.
9. While the biscuits are baking, toss sliced strawberries with 2 tablespoons of sugar in a bowl. Let them sit and macerate until the biscuits are ready.
10. Once the biscuits are done, let them cool slightly before assembling the strawberry shortcakes.
11. To assemble, split each biscuit in half horizontally. Top the bottom half with a spoonful of macerated strawberries and whipped cream. Place the top half of the biscuit over the filling.
12. Serve immediately.

Nutritional Information (per serving):

- Calories: 350
- Protein: 5g
- Total Fats: 16g
- Fiber: 2g
- Carbohydrates: 45g

Chapter 8: Dehydrate Recipes

Dehydrated Apple Slices

Time to Prepare: 15 minutes
Cooking Time: 4 hours
Servings: 4

Ingredients:

- 4 apples (any variety)
- 1 tablespoon lemon juice
- Cinnamon (optional)

Instructions List:

1. Wash and core the apples. Thinly slice them into rounds, about 1/8 inch thick.
2. Place the apple slices in a bowl and toss them with lemon juice to prevent browning.
3. Arrange the apple slices in a single layer on the dehydrator trays, ensuring they do not overlap.
4. Optionally, sprinkle cinnamon over the apple slices for added flavor.
5. Insert the dehydrator trays into the Ninja Foodi Digital Air Fryer Oven.
6. Set the dehydration function to 135°F and let the apples dehydrate for 4 hours.
7. Check the apples periodically during the dehydration process and rotate the trays if necessary for even drying.
8. Once the apple slices are dehydrated to your desired texture (they should be dry and leathery), remove them from the dehydrator.
9. Let the apple slices cool completely before storing them in an airtight container.

Nutritional Information (per serving):

- Calories: 70
- Protein: 0g
- Total Fats: 0g
- Fiber: 3g
- Carbohydrates: 19g

Crispy Kale Chips

Time to Prepare: 10 minutes
Cooking Time: 25 minutes
Servings: 4

Ingredients:

- 1 bunch kale, stems removed and leaves torn into bite-sized pieces
- 1 tablespoon olive oil
- 1/2 teaspoon of salt
- 1/4 teaspoon of black pepper
- Optional seasonings: garlic powder, paprika, nutritional yeast

Instructions List:

1. Wash the kale leaves thoroughly and dry them completely using a salad spinner or paper towels.
2. In a large bowl, toss the kale leaves with olive oil, salt, and black pepper until evenly coated.
3. If desired, sprinkle the kale leaves with additional seasonings like garlic powder, paprika, or nutritional yeast for extra flavor.
4. Arrange the seasoned kale leaves in a single layer on the dehydrator trays, ensuring they do not overlap.
5. Insert the dehydrator trays into the Ninja Foodi Digital Air Fryer Oven.
6. Set the dehydration function to 135°F and let the kale dehydrate for 25 minutes.
7. Check the kale chips periodically during the dehydration process and rotate the trays if necessary for even drying.
8. Once the kale chips are crispy and dry, remove them from the dehydrator.
9. Let the kale chips cool completely before serving or storing them in an airtight container.

Nutritional Information (per serving):

- Calories: 50

- Protein: 2g
- Total Fats: 3g
- Fiber: 2g
- Carbohydrates: 5g

Sun-dried Tomatoes

Time to Prepare: 10 minutes
Cooking Time: 6 hours
Servings: 8

Ingredients:

- 2 pounds ripe tomatoes
- Salt, to taste
- Olive oil (optional)

Instructions List:

1. Wash the tomatoes and pat them dry with paper towels.
2. Slice the tomatoes into thin rounds, approximately 1/4 inch thick.
3. Arrange the tomato slices in a single layer on the dehydrator trays, ensuring they do not touch each other.
4. Sprinkle salt lightly over the tomato slices.
5. Insert the dehydrator trays into the Ninja Foodi Digital Air Fryer Oven.
6. Set the dehydration function to 135°F and let the tomatoes dehydrate for 6 hours.
7. Check the tomatoes periodically during the dehydration process and rotate the trays if necessary for even drying.
8. Once the tomatoes are dried to your desired texture, remove them from the dehydrator.
9. If desired, drizzle olive oil over the dried tomatoes for added flavor and moisture.
10. Let the sun-dried tomatoes cool completely before storing them in an airtight container.

Nutritional Information (per serving):

- Calories: 30
- Protein: 1g
- Total Fats: 0g
- Fiber: 1g
- Carbohydrates: 7g

Homemade Fruit Leather

Time to Prepare: 15 minutes
Cooking Time: 4 hours
Servings: 6

Ingredients:

- 4 cups of chopped mixed fruit (such as strawberries, peaches, and apples)
- 2 tablespoons honey or maple syrup (optional)
- 1 tablespoon lemon juice

Instructions List:

1. Preheat the Ninja Foodi Digital Air Fryer Oven to 135°F.
2. Place the chopped mixed fruit in a blender or food processor. Blend until smooth.
3. If desired, add honey or maple syrup to the fruit puree for sweetness.
4. Add lemon juice to the fruit puree and blend again to combine.
5. Line the dehydrator trays with parchment paper or silicone mats.
6. Pour the fruit puree onto the prepared trays, spreading it evenly with a spatula to create a thin layer.
7. Insert the dehydrator trays into the Ninja Foodi Digital Air Fryer Oven.
8. Set the dehydration function to 135°F and let the fruit leather dehydrate for 4 hours.
9. Check the fruit leather periodically during the dehydration process to ensure even drying.
10. Once the fruit leather is dry and no longer sticky to the touch, remove it from the dehydrator.
11. Let the fruit leather cool completely before cutting it into strips or shapes.
12. Roll the fruit leather strips in parchment paper or plastic wrap for storage.

Nutritional Information (per serving):

- Calories: 80
- Protein: 1g
- Total Fats: 0g
- Fiber: 2g
- Carbohydrates: 20g

Dehydrated Banana Chips

Time to Prepare: 10 minutes
Cooking Time: 6 hours
Servings: 4

Ingredients:

- 4 ripe bananas
- Lemon juice (optional)

Instructions List:

1. Peel the bananas and slice them into rounds, about 1/8 inch thick.
2. If desired, dip the banana slices in lemon juice to prevent browning.
3. Arrange the banana slices in a single layer on the dehydrator trays, ensuring they do not overlap.
4. Insert the dehydrator trays into the Ninja Foodi Digital Air Fryer Oven.
5. Set the dehydration function to 135°F and let the bananas dehydrate for 6 hours.
6. Check the banana chips periodically during the dehydration process and rotate the trays if necessary for even drying.
7. Once the banana chips are dry and crisp, remove them from the dehydrator.
8. Let the banana chips cool completely before storing them in an airtight container.

Nutritional Information (per serving):

- Calories: 110
- Protein: 1g
- Total Fats: 0g
- Fiber: 2g
- Carbohydrates: 29g

Dehydrated Bell Pepper Strips

Time to Prepare: 15 minutes
Cooking Time: 6 hours
Servings: 4

Ingredients:

- 2 large bell peppers (any color)

Instructions List:

1. Wash the bell peppers and pat them dry with paper towels.
2. Remove the stems and seeds from the bell peppers.
3. Slice the bell peppers into thin strips, about 1/4 inch wide.
4. Arrange the bell pepper strips in a single layer on the dehydrator trays, ensuring they do not overlap.
5. Insert the dehydrator trays into the Ninja Foodi Digital Air Fryer Oven.
6. Set the dehydration function to 135°F and let the bell peppers dehydrate for 6 hours.
7. Check the bell pepper strips periodically during the dehydration process and rotate the trays if necessary for even drying.
8. Once the bell pepper strips are completely dry and crispy, remove them from the dehydrator.
9. Let the bell pepper strips cool completely before storing them in an airtight container.

Nutritional Information (per serving):

- Calories: 20
- Protein: 1g
- Total Fats: 0g
- Fiber: 2g
- Carbohydrates: 5g

Herb Medley

Time to Prepare: 10 minutes
Cooking Time: 3 hours
Servings: 4

Ingredients:

- Assorted fresh herbs (such as rosemary, thyme, oregano, and sage)

Instructions List:

1. Wash the fresh herbs and pat them dry with paper towels.
2. Remove the leaves from the stems and discard any tough stems.
3. Arrange the herb leaves in a single layer on the dehydrator trays, ensuring they do not overlap.
4. Insert the dehydrator trays into the Ninja Foodi Digital Air Fryer Oven.
5. Set the dehydration function to 95°F and let the herbs dehydrate for 3 hours.
6. Check the herbs periodically during the dehydration process and rotate the trays if necessary for even drying.
7. Once the herbs are completely dry and brittle, remove them from the dehydrator.
8. Let the herbs cool completely before crumbling them or storing them whole in an airtight container.

Nutritional Information (per serving):

- Calories: 5
- Protein: 0g
- Total Fats: 0g
- Fiber: 1g
- Carbohydrates: 1g

Beef Jerky

Time to Prepare: 20 minutes
Cooking Time: 4 hours
Servings: 4

Ingredients:

- 1 pound beef (preferably lean cuts like flank steak or sirloin), thinly sliced against the grain
- 1/4 cup of soy sauce
- 2 tablespoons Worcestershire sauce
- 1 tablespoon honey or maple syrup
- 1 teaspoon of garlic powder
- 1 teaspoon of onion powder
- 1/2 teaspoon of black pepper
- 1/2 teaspoon of smoked paprika
- 1/4 teaspoon of cayenne pepper (optional)

Instructions List:

1. In a bowl, combine soy sauce, Worcestershire sauce, honey or maple syrup, garlic powder, onion powder, black pepper, smoked paprika, and cayenne pepper (if using). Stir until well fat.
2. Place the thinly sliced beef in a resealable plastic bag or shallow dish.
3. Pour the marinade over the beef, ensuring all slices are coated. Seal the bag or cover the dish and refrigerate for at least 2 hours, or preferably overnight.
4. Preheat the Ninja Foodi Digital Air Fryer Oven to 160°F for dehydrating.
5. Remove the marinated beef from the refrigerator and drain off any excess marinade.
6. Arrange the beef slices in a single layer on the dehydrator trays, leaving space between each slice for air circulation.
7. Insert the dehydrator trays into the oven and dehydrate the beef at 160°F for 4 hours, or until the beef is dry and chewy.
8. Check the beef jerky periodically during the dehydration process and rotate the trays if necessary for even drying.
9. Once the beef jerky is done, remove it from the oven and let it cool completely.
10. Store the beef jerky in an airtight container or resealable bags.

Nutritional Information (per serving):

- Calories: 180
- Protein: 20g
- Total Fats: 9g
- Fiber: 0g
- Carbohydrates: 4g

Mushroom Crisps

Time to Prepare: 15 minutes
Cooking Time: 4 hours
Servings: 4

Ingredients:

- 8 ounces mushrooms, thinly sliced
- Olive oil spray
- Salt, to taste
- Black pepper, to taste
- Garlic powder, to taste (optional)
- Onion powder, to taste (optional)

Instructions List:

1. Preheat the Ninja Foodi Digital Air Fryer Oven to 135°F for dehydrating.
2. Arrange the thinly sliced mushrooms in a single layer on the dehydrator trays, ensuring they do not overlap.
3. Lightly spray the mushroom slices with olive oil spray.
4. Season the mushrooms with salt, black pepper, and any optional seasonings like garlic powder or onion powder.
5. Insert the dehydrator trays into the oven and dehydrate the mushrooms at 135°F for 4 hours.
6. Check the mushrooms periodically during the dehydration process and rotate the trays if necessary for even drying.
7. Once the mushrooms are completely dry and crispy, remove them from the dehydrator.
8. Let the mushroom crisps cool completely before storing them in an airtight container.
9. Enjoy as a healthy snack or use as a topping for salads or soups.

Nutritional Information (per serving):

- Calories: 20
- Protein: 2g
- Total Fats: 0g
- Fiber: 1g
- Carbohydrates: 3g

MEASUREMENT CONVERSION TABLE

Measurement	Imperial (US)	Metric
Volume		
1 teaspoon	1 tsp	5 milliliters
1 tablespoon	1 tbsp	15 milliliters
1 fluid ounce	1 fl oz	30 milliliters
1 cup	1 cup	240 milliliters
1 pint	1 pt	473 milliliters
1 quart	1 qt	0.95 liters
1 gallon	1 gal	3.8 liters
Weight		
1 ounce	1 oz	28 grams
1 pound	1 lb	454 grams
Temperature		
32°F	32°F	0°C
212°F	212°F	100°C
Other		
1 stick of butter	1 stick	113 grams

CONCLUSION

Thank you for choosing the Ninja Foodi Digital Air Fryer Oven Cookbook to elevate your culinary adventures. This versatile appliance has unlocked a world of possibilities, allowing you to create a variety of delicious dishes with ease and convenience. From crispy appetizers to delectable desserts, we've covered a wide range of recipes that cater to different tastes and dietary preferences.

We hope that these recipes have inspired you to experiment with new flavors and techniques, making the most of your Ninja Foodi Digital Air Fryer Oven. Whether you're a seasoned cook or just starting out, these dishes are designed to be approachable and rewarding, bringing joy to your kitchen and dining table.

Remember, the key to great cooking lies in creativity and passion. Don't hesitate to adapt these recipes to your personal preferences or to explore new ingredients and methods. The Ninja Foodi Digital Air Fryer Oven is a powerful tool that can help you achieve culinary excellence, one meal at a time.

Happy cooking!

RECIPES INDEX

Made in the USA
Las Vegas, NV
23 November 2024